15-minute cook

15-minutecook

Anne Willan

Photography by Sara Taylor

Quadrille

To the Cherniavsky kitchen trio,
Mark, Simon and Emma

Both metric and imperial quantities are given. Use either
all metric or all imperial, as the two are not necessarily
interchangeable.

Publishing Director: Anne Furniss
Art Director: Mary Evans
Project Manager: Lewis Esson
Editor: Janet Illsley
Photography: Sara Taylor
Styling: Penny Markham
Food Styling: Roz Denny, and Jane Suthering
  assisted by Emma Patmore
Design Assistant: Sarah Emery
Production: Sarah Tucker

First published in 2000 by
Quadrille Publishing Limited
5th floor, Alhambra House
Charing Cross Road
London WC2H 0LS

This paperback edition first published in 2003
10 9 8 7 6 5 4 3 2

Based on material already published as
In and Out of the Kitchen in 15 Minutes or Less

Text © 1995 and 2000 Anne Willan Inc.

Cataloguing in Publication Data: a catalogue record for this
book is available from the British Library

ISBN 1 844000 31 1

contents

introduction

None of us has much time to spend in the kitchen, yet we all love to eat well. The recipes in this book are my personal solution to the problem, the way I cook myself. With all of them you'll be in and out of the kitchen in 15 minutes or less, free to relax while the dish simmers, bakes or chills. For some, you needn't wait at all but can go straight to the table.

You'll see at once that this is real food, made with market-fresh ingredients. Now that there's so much fresh produce available all year round, and so many exotic flavourings which were not in our shops a decade ago, we have plenty to play with. It's the way I've been cooking for years, ever since I started balancing a husband, two children and a busy professional life.

There's no need to compromise with ready-prepared foods which are often expensive and always inferior in taste.

Throughout the book, I've concentrated on dishes which are substantial enough to anchor a menu with little or no accompaniment. What won't you find here? No breads and few pastries or cakes, as they require far too much work. Roast meats need basting and are finished with a sauce or gravy, so don't meet our '15 minutes then relax' rule. However, I think you'll be surprised by the range of possible dishes.

This is my style of cooking and my kind of food. With this book I welcome you into my kitchen, hoping you enjoy it as much as I do. All I'm asking for is 15 minutes of your time!

How to use this book

Wherever possible, the recipes in this book try to give you some background, for instance advice on choosing ingredients and finding substitutes, or what to look out for in a tricky technique. If you've already been successful with a dish, for a repeat performance you should only need to consult the ingredient list.

Quantities are geared to serve four. If you're a smaller party – two, or even solo – you're not going to save much time by reducing quantities, and you may compromise results as ingredient amounts do not necessarily change in direct proportion to servings. You'll be much better off enjoying a few leftovers the following day. For flexibility, I've tried to indicate dishes which reheat well and those which are easy to make in large quantities.

In saving time, we have to cut some corners. Vegetables are rarely peeled, so you'll find lots of earthy texture and taste. If produce is available in your market already washed, go for it. As I often suggest in my recipe introductions, wherever possible get the fishmonger or butcher to fillet, clean and slice things for you.

Quite a number of recipes call for a food processor or mixer – both great time-savers. I'd opt for a different recipe if you don't have either machine. The microwave I find less useful, but I do suggest it as an alternative in a dozen or so recipes where you can save significant time without spoiling the outcome.

Finally, you'll find that there are two procedures that simply cannot be hurried – the heating of the oven and boiling a pan of water, so quite often I ask you to do these things before actually starting the recipe.

The well-stocked store cupboard

Everyone's idea of a well-stocked store-cupboard differs, and here is mine. All the items can be kept for weeks or months so they are true store-cupboard ingredients. I'm not suggesting by any means that you need all of the following ingredients. They are food for thought before we go into the kitchen.

Basics

Even the most modest college dorm or bachelor studio surely stocks: salt, black pepper, flour, granulated sugar, vegetable oil, tea and coffee. Add some options with ground white pepper, black peppercorns, brown and caster sugar.

Flavourings

Here's where the fun begins. Vinegars can run to red and white wine, cider, rice, raspberry and balsamic. Oils may include olive, walnut, and dark sesame oil for an Oriental touch. For salty and piquant flavour, there are soy, Worcestershire and Tabasco sauces, capers, anchovies, sun-dried tomatoes, horseradish and Dijon mustard, before we even look at Oriental possibilities, like oyster, fish and plum sauces. For desserts, don't forget vanilla essence and pods.

Spices and herbs

Aromatic spices start with nutmeg, ground and stick cinnamon, whole and ground allspice and coriander, ground and seed cumin. For colour, look to saffron, turmeric and paprika. For heat you need dry mustard, ginger and the chilli family – dried pepper flakes, cayenne pepper and chilli paste. As for dried herbs, I find only a few retain their aroma – bay, rosemary, thyme and sage do well. For other herbs, fresh sprigs have far more flavour and will keep for about a week in the refrigerator. I don't go much for mixes, except for Provençal herbs and curry powder.

Introduction

Grains and Pasta

Our family tastes turn to grains rather than pasta, so we rarely stock more than: dried spaghetti, macaroni or fusilli, tagliatelle and perhaps some Oriental rice noodles. We're much more adventurous with grains, so you can count on finding cracked wheat, bulgur, kasha, couscous and polenta among the rice – long-grain white rice, basmati, wild and probably brown as well. Add a few oddments, such as lentils and rolled oats and you've got the basis of dozens of meals right there.

Dried fruits, nuts and preserves

Here's where sweetness and texture come from, starting with: raisins, prunes, dried apricots, figs and dates, and my favourite candied orange and ginger for cakes. My cupboard is always full of nuts – walnuts, pecans, hazelnuts (preferably peeled as well as shelled), shelled and blanched pistachios, pine nuts, and a slew of almonds, whole, blanched, slivered and ground. Peanut butter, too. This is the place to mention redcurrant jelly and apricot jam, for glazing fruit tarts, plus a pot of citrus marmalade and hopefully some home-made jam. Last, and most important of all, are honey and bittersweet chocolate, the basis of so many contemporary desserts.

Cans

You'll find very few cans in our house, just several of whole tomatoes (preferably plum) and some tomato paste, in a tube so it keeps better after opening. I find canned white kidney beans quite useful for adding body to vegetable soup, with some cans of low-salt veal and chicken stock for emergency. That's it.

The freezer

In our freezer there's always a back-up supply of fresh tagliatelle, butter and grated Parmesan or Gruyère cheese. We add our own fresh peas, green beans and other garden vegetables, but the only commercially frozen produce I ever buy is leaf spinach and raspberries. Add sliced white or brown bread (for toast), filo pastry (too difficult to make fresh), thinly sliced bacon (because we love it), and some good ice-cream.

Fresh produce

The following items will last a week or two, depending on the temperature of your kitchen. In your standby vegetable rack I would hope to find potatoes and roots such as carrots, and perhaps turnip, leeks or celery. The onion family – Spanish onions, sweet red, spring onions or white onions for salad, and garlic – are indispensable. Some shallots would be helpful, as would a chunk of fresh root ginger. And you must include some citrus fruit – oranges, lemons and limes.

The refrigerator

We look here for dairy produce, including butter, milk, cream, eggs, yogurt, sour cream and cream cheese.

The drinks cupboard

Starting with red and white wine, we move to fortified wines such as Marsala, Madeira, sherry and Port. A dash of spirits – Cognac, rum, or whisky and maybe a lesser-known type such as Calvados or Pernod – lifts many a ragout and sauce (only vodka has little to offer in the way of background taste). White alcohols such as kirsch and poire (pear brandy) do well in desserts, as do liqueurs like orange-based Grand Marnier or Cointreau.

Introduction

Chapter 1

off to a

quick start

Rarely do we forgo a starter at home, even if it's only a green salad sprinkled with cheese or chopped walnuts. I think of a starter as setting the stage for a meal, raising expectations and leading without fuss into the main course. Or that's the way it should be.

As always, I like to be organized. Each recipe has its place. The starter must be easy to make ahead, so I can focus on the main dish without interruption. Smoked Salmon or Mackerel Rillettes, or a Chicken Liver and Apple Mousse are ideal for a party. On a warm evening, we may relax by ourselves with a chilled Melon Salad with Balsamic Vinegar, while on winter days, Italian Escarole Soup makes a welcome opening. Both take less than 10 minutes to prepare and are ready to eat almost at once. As a Saturday treat, Potted Shrimps are a weakness of ours, with a glass of good Chardonnay.

Good appetizers are so attractive that in restaurants I don't hesitate to have two, or even three, forgetting the main course altogether. I wouldn't suggest you do that here unless you have time to spare. You will find, however, that recipes such as Salmon Carpaccio can form a pleasant summer meal if you increase the quantities and supplement with a green salad and a fresh loaf of your favourite bread.

Red wine gazpacho

- 2 slices of white bread
- 500 g /1 lb very ripe large tomatoes
- 1 red pepper
- ½ medium cucumber
- 1 garlic clove
- 4 tablespoons olive oil
- 125 ml /4 fl oz red wine
- 3 tablespoons red wine vinegar, or to taste
- pinch of sugar
- salt and freshly ground black pepper
- ice cubes, to serve

Flavourful ripe tomatoes are essential for this refreshing, chilled Spanish soup. Fresh tomatoes at their peak are the best choice, but canned tomatoes are a time-saving option.

1 Put the bread in a small bowl, pour on 250 ml /8 fl oz cold water and leave to soak.

2 Halve, core and deseed the tomatoes and red pepper, then cut into large chunks. Peel the cucumber, reserving 4 thin strips of peel for garnish. Halve the cucumber lengthwise, scoop out the seeds, then cut the flesh into chunks. Peel the garlic.

3 Purée half of the tomatoes, pepper and cucumber in a food processor until smooth, then transfer to a large bowl.

4 Squeeze the soaked bread to remove excess water. Purée with the rest of the vegetables, the garlic and olive oil; add to the bowl.

5 Stir in the wine, vinegar, sugar and seasoning to taste. Cover and chill for at least 2 hours, or up to 24 hours.

6 Stir the gazpacho: it should be quite thick, but can be thinned with a little water. Check the seasoning and add a little more vinegar if required. Spoon into serving bowls, add ice cubes and garnish with knotted strips of cucumber peel.

time in kitchen 9 minutes   serves **4**

chilling time 2–24 hours

This soup is delicious served topped with a sprinkling of grated Parmesan cheese. If escarole – also sold as Batavian endive – is not available, you can substitute curly endive.

1 Bring the stock to the boil in a covered pan. While it heats, peel and chop the garlic.

2 Heat the oil in a soup pan, add the garlic and cook gently for 1-2 minutes until soft and golden.

3 Meanwhile, discard the tough outer leaves from the escarole, trim the stem and separate the inner leaves; wash if necessary. Chop fairly coarsely, depending on the texture required. Add to the soup pan with a little seasoning and sauté for 1-2 minutes.

4 Add the boiling stock, cover and simmer for 10-15 minutes, until the escarole is tender. (Or microwave on high in a covered bowl for 5 minutes). Meanwhile, roughly shred the basil.

5 Stir in the beans with their liquid and bring just back to the boil. Stir in the basil, check the seasoning and serve.

Italian escarole soup

1 litre /1¾ pt chicken or vegetable stock

2 garlic cloves

2 tablespoons olive oil

1 small head of escarole (about 500 g /1 lb)

small handful of basil leaves

250 g /8 oz can of cooked white kidney beans

salt and freshly ground black pepper

time in kitchen **7 minutes**   serves **4**

total cooking time 10–15 minutes (5–6 in microwave)

Chicken liver & apple mousse

125 g /4 oz chicken livers

60 g /2 oz unsalted butter

1 dessert apple

2 shallots

2 tablespoons Calvados or Cognac

salt and freshly ground black pepper

This mousse is easy to make in larger quantities and keeps well, for up to 3 days if sealed with a thin layer of melted butter. French bread is the appropriate accompaniment.

1 Cut each chicken liver into 2 or 3 pieces, discarding any membrane. Pat dry with kitchen paper.

2 Melt half the butter in a frying pan. Add the livers, season and sauté over medium heat. Meanwhile peel, quarter and core the apple. Thinly slice the apple quarters into the pan and stir to mix with the livers.

3 Peel the shallots, slice them thinly and stir into the pan. Increase the heat to high and cook for 2-3 minutes until the livers are well browned on the outside but still pink in the centre.

4 Take the pan off the heat, pour in the Calvados or Cognac and set alight. When the flame has died down, tip the contents of the pan into a food processor. Add the remaining butter and purée until smooth.

5 Season to taste, adding plenty of pepper. Spoon into an earthenware pot or individual dishes and smooth the surface. Cover and chill for at least 4 hours before serving.

time in kitchen **10 minutes**   serves **4-6**

total cooking time 5–6 minutes | chilling time at least 4 hours

Angels & devils on **horseback**

8 thin slices of bacon
(about 250 g / ½ lb)

8 shelled medium oysters
(about 100 g / 3¼ oz)

8 pitted ready-to-eat prunes
(about 60 g / 2 oz)

4 slices of white bread

30 g / 1 oz unsalted butter

½ teaspoon Worcestershire
sauce, or to taste

Bacon rolls filled with oysters and prunes and set on toast make a tempting cocktail savoury or starter. Scallops are alternative angels to oysters, or chicken livers may replace prunes as devils.

1 Preheat the grill and cover the grill rack with foil. Cut the bacon slices in half. Roll each oyster in a bacon slice and spear with a wooden cocktail stick. Repeat with the prunes.

2 Set the rolls on the grill rack and grill about 5 cm / 2 in from the heat for about 2 minutes. Turn the skewers and grill for a further 2-3 minutes until the bacon is crisp and brown, but the oysters are still soft.

3 Meanwhile, toast the bread in a toaster. Melt the butter and flavour with the Worcestershire sauce. Trim the crusts from the toast and halve each slice diagonally. Brush with the flavoured butter.

4 Set 2 toast triangles on each warmed serving plate. Top with the angels and devils and serve very hot.

time in kitchen **10 minutes**   serves **4**

total cooking time 8 minutes

500 g /1 lb peeled cooked
shrimps or prawns

½ teaspoon freshly grated
nutmeg, or to taste

small pinch of cayenne
pepper

75 g /2½ oz unsalted butter

salt and freshly ground
black pepper

1 lemon, cut into wedges,
to serve

Potted shrimps

Spice and nutty brown butter accentuate the sweet flavour of shellfish to delicious effect. Ordinary prawns are fine, but use freshly cooked rather than frozen ones. Pink baby shrimps are even better, and best of all are grey or bay shrimps. Potted shrimps are good hot or cold, and can be kept in the refrigerator for up to 2 days.

1 If using prawns, coarsely chop in the food processor; baby shrimps should be left whole. Put the prawns or shrimps in a bowl and season with the nutmeg, cayenne, salt and plenty of black pepper. Stir well.

2 Melt the butter in a wok and place over a medium heat for 20-30 seconds, until it starts to colour slightly.

3 Increase the heat, add the prawns or shrimps and stir-fry over a high heat for 1-2 minutes, until starting to brown.

4 Take off the heat and season with salt, pepper and more nutmeg to taste – they should be quite spicy.

5 Serve hot or cold, with lemon wedges, accompanied by crusty wholewheat bread or toast. If you want to enjoy them cold, turn into an earthenware pot or individual ramekins and chill for at least 2 hours until the butter sets.

time in kitchen **7-8 minutes**   serves **4**

total cooking time 2 minutes

Smoked salmon rillettes

These rillettes combine smoked with fresh salmon. Serve them with melba toast or thinly sliced wholewheat bread.

1 Put 15 g /½ oz of the butter and 3 tablespoons of water in a frying pan over medium heat. With a sharp knife, split the salmon fillet horizontally in two.

2 Add the fresh and smoked salmon to the pan and coat with the liquid. Cover and cook gently for 3-4 minutes, until the fish flakes easily.

3 Cream the remaining butter in a mixer fitted with the 'K' hook. Meanwhile, cut 4 slices from 1 lemon half; squeeze the juice from the other half.

4 Drain the salmon and add to the mixer. With the motor on low speed, add the cayenne, nutmeg, black pepper and lemon juice. Work the mixture for 2-3 minutes, to a coarse purée. Check the seasoning.

5 Transfer to a bowl, cover and chill for at least 2 hours until the butter sets slightly. Rillettes can be kept in the refrigerator for up to 2 days, but bring them to room temperature to soften and stir before serving.

6 Spoon the rillettes into ramekins or small dishes. Top with lemon slices and serve with toast or bread.

Smoked mackerel rillettes

Substitute 375 g /12 oz smoked mackerel fillets (preferably peppered) for the smoked and fresh salmon. Soften them skin-side up in the liquid for 2 minutes only. Drain, then flake, discarding skin and any bones. Continue as above.

125 g /4 oz unsalted butter, softened

125 g /4 oz boneless skinless salmon fillet

125 g /4 oz smoked salmon, sliced or in pieces

1 lemon, halved

small pinch of cayenne pepper

¼ teaspoon freshly grated nutmeg

freshly ground black pepper

time in kitchen **9 minutes**   serves **4**

total cooking time 3–4 minutes

Salmon carpaccio

500 g /1 lb fillet of salmon with skin

2 lemons

4 tablespoons olive oil

small bunch of chives

2 tablespoons capers

3–4 sprigs of flat-leaf parsley

salt and freshly ground black pepper

Marinating raw salmon in lemon juice with aromatic flavourings enhances the taste, while the acid whitens and slightly 'cooks' the fish. The salmon must be very fresh.

1 Remove any residual bones from the salmon with tweezers. With a very sharp knife, cut the salmon into wafer-thin diagonal slices off the skin, working away from you towards the tail of the fillet. Lay the slices on 4 large serving plates as you go.

2 Halve the lemon. Squeeze the juice from 1 lemon half over each serving and drizzle with olive oil. Brush the lemon juice and oil over the salmon to coat evenly.

3 Using scissors, snip the chives over the fish. Rinse the capers, pat dry and scatter these over. Chop the parsley leaves, sprinkle them over and season lightly with salt and generously with pepper to taste.

4 Cover the plates with cling film and leave to marinate in the refrigerator for 15-30 minutes. Don't leave the salmon much longer or it will lose its fresh flavour.

time in kitchen **10 minutes**   serves **4**

marinating time 15–30 minutes

These mushrooms can be marinated up to 3 days in advance. Serve with focaccia to mop up the tasty juices.

1 Tie the peppercorns, bay leaves, thyme and parsley in a square of muslin, using cotton string. Pour 250 ml /8 fl oz water into a sauté pan and add the coriander seeds, wine and muslin bag. Bring to the boil.

2 Strain the juice from the tomatoes into the pan. Chop the tomatoes and add them too. Add the juice from 1 lemon, with a little salt. Peel the onions, cut each into 8 wedges and add to the pan.

3 Trim off the mushroom stems, halve or quarter any larger mushrooms, then add them all to the pan. Simmer for 20-25 minutes until the onions and mushrooms are tender and the marinade is reduced and well flavoured.

4 Adjust the seasoning, allow to cool, then chill for at least 1 hour. Meanwhile, thinly slice half of the remaining lemon; squeeze the juice from the other half.

5 Just before serving, discard the muslin bag of herbs from the marinated mushrooms. Add the lemon juice and freshly ground pepper. Check the seasoning again – the marinade should be quite piquant. Serve the mushrooms topped with lemon slices.

Marinated mushrooms

1 tablespoon black peppercorns

3 bay leaves

2-3 sprigs of fresh or dried thyme

3-4 sprigs of parsley

2 tablespoons coriander seeds

125 ml /4 fl oz dry white wine

250 g /8 oz can whole plum tomatoes

2 lemons

3 onions

500 g /1 lb button mushrooms

salt and freshly ground black pepper

time in kitchen 10 minutes   serves **4**

total cooking time 20–25 minutes

Melon salad with **balsamic vinegar**

5 tablespoons balsamic vinegar

4 teaspoons sugar, or more to taste

250 g /½ lb raspberries

2 small ripe melons (about 500 g /1 lb each)

Fragrance is the most reliable indicator of a freshly picked melon at its peak of ripeness. Look for a large (rather than small) round scar at the flower end too - this denotes a female melon, which is the juicier of the species. When pressed gently, this area should 'give' slightly.

1 Mix the vinegar and sugar together in a bowl. Pick over the raspberries and wash only if necessary. Add them to the vinegar, toss gently and leave to macerate a few minutes.

2 Trim a thin slice from both ends of each melon, so the halves will sit flat, then cut the melons in half. Scoop out the seeds with a spoon and discard.

3 Pile the raspberries and juice into the melon halves, cover loosely with cling film and chill for at least 20 minutes, or up to 2 hours before serving.

time in kitchen **6 minutes**   serves **4**

chilling time 20 minutes – 2 hours

wholes

1 2 3 4 5 6 7 8 9 10 11 12 13 14 15 1 2 3 4 5 6 7 8 9 10 11 12 13 14 15 1 2 3 4 5 6 7 8 9 10 11 12 13 14 15

in one

When I'm planning a menu, here's where I begin. The recipes in this chapter are designed to be a full meal, needing – at most – a simple accompaniment of pasta, rice, boiled potatoes, bread or a green salad. Dishes such as Tajine of Chicken with Aubergine and Breton Chaudrée are full meals in themselves. Quite a challenge for only 15 minutes' work!

To me, fish is often a first choice as it cooks quickly and suits simple treatment. Most of the ideas here suit a variety of fish, and you'll find others in the Fifteen Minutes to Table chapter. It's less the actual fish than its type that is important: rich-fleshed, like salmon; fine-textured, such as sole; or firm, such as tuna. Just snap up whatever is sparkling fresh.

Turning to the chicken recipes you can choose between chicken breasts, quick-cooking wings, and even a whole Chicken in a Salt Crust – enormous fun, though it takes a while to cook. Aside from a plain steak, meat in 15 minutes is more of a challenge, but Baked Ham with Apples and Cream doesn't take long to put together for the oven, nor does Roast Pork Loin with Baker's Potatoes.

This chapter is just a start for main-course ideas. If you're in a hurry, turn to Fifteen Minutes to Table for dishes that are ready at once. If you're looking for something lighter, turn to Speedy Salads and Not Quite Vegetarian for a selection of favourites of mine.

250 ml /8 fl oz yogurt

12-16 chicken wings
(about 1.4 kg /3 lb)

1 tablespoon olive oil

1 onion

2 large beefsteak tomatoes

125 ml /4 fl oz double cream

salt and freshly ground
black pepper

Coating meat with seasoned yogurt before cooking is a Middle-Eastern trick which imparts flavour and enriches the colour of these chicken wings on baking.

1 Preheat the oven to its highest setting. Mix the yogurt, 1 teaspoon salt and ½ teaspoon pepper in a large bowl. Add the chicken and toss to coat. Set aside until the oven is hot.

2 Place the chicken wings on a foil-lined baking sheet and spoon over any remaining marinade. Bake in the oven for 15-20 minutes, turning halfway through cooking.

3 Meanwhile, heat the oil in a small frying pan. Peel the onion, halve and thinly slice. Add to the oil, season and cook gently to soften.

Chicken wings with tomatoes in cream

time in kitchen **11 minutes**

total cooking time 15–20 minutes

serves **4**

4 Core and halve the tomatoes. Sprinkle the cut surfaces with salt and pepper.

5 Increase heat under the pan to medium and move the onions to one side. Add the tomatoes, cut side down, and cook for 2-3 minutes. Turn the tomatoes and cook for a further 2 minutes.

6 Stir the cream into the onions and spread them over the base of the pan. Let bubble to reduce and thicken slightly. Cover and set aside.

7 When the chicken wings are brown and tender, reheat the tomatoes. Transfer the tomatoes and sauce to a platter and top with the chicken.

1 oven-ready chicken (about 1.8 kg /4 lb)

2.75 kg /6 lb kosher or sea salt

Chicken in a salt crust

This is the only recipe I know that calls for just two ingredients – chicken and coarse salt. The chicken is baked in a salt coat, retaining its juiciness and full flavour. Kosher salt is preferred to sea salt, as it is milder and less expensive than speciality salts like Maldon. Serve with Provençal Tricolor (page 101), or buttery new potatoes with parsley.

1 Preheat the oven to its highest possible setting. Truss the chicken with string to hold it in a compact shape. Spread a 2 cm /¾ in layer of salt in a deep heatproof casserole. Set the chicken on top and scatter over the remaining salt, so the bird is encased in a 2 cm /¾ in thick layer.

2 Cover with the lid and bake for 1¼ –1½ hours. To test, insert a meat thermometer through the salt crust into the thickest part of the thigh of the chicken: it should read at least 75°C/170°F. If not, cook for a further 10–15 minutes, then test again.

3 Lift the chicken out of the casserole and discard the salt. Use kitchen paper to rub off any crystals that stick. Set the bird on a platter and carve it at the table.

time in kitchen 5 minutes **serves 3-4**

total cooking time 1¼–1½ hours

You can use any part of the chicken in this Indonesian recipe: breasts, thighs, wings, or the whole bird cut into 8 pieces as I suggest here. The sauce gives the chicken a delicious tang and boiled rice is the ideal foil.

1 Preheat the oven to 190°C/375°F/gas 5. Peel the shallots and cut each into 2–3 pieces. Peel the garlic. Trim the lemon grass, discarding the tough outer leaves and cut into 2–3 pieces.

2 Put the shallots, garlic, lemon grass, nuts, turmeric, coriander, chilli and half the oil in a food processor and work to a purée.

3 Put the remaining oil in a sauté pan or shallow flameproof casserole, large enough to hold all the chicken pieces in a single layer. Add the puréed mixture and cook, stirring constantly, for 1-2 minutes.

4 Add the chicken pieces, skin side down, and cook for 2-3 minutes, turning occasionally to ensure they are well coated with the spice mix. Stir in the coconut milk and bring back to the boil.

5 Cover and cook in the oven for 40-50 minutes, until the chicken pieces are very tender and the sauce is reduced and thickened. Check seasoning and serve the chicken from the casserole, or transfer it to a serving dish.

Chicken in chilli coconut sauce

3 shallots

2 garlic cloves

2 stalks of fresh lemon grass

8 macadamia nuts or
16 blanched almonds

2 teaspoons turmeric

2 teaspoons ground coriander

1 teaspoon ground dried hot
red chilli pepper, or to taste

5 tablespoons groundnut
or vegetable oil

1 oven-ready chicken (about
1.8 kg /4 lb), cut into 8 pieces

500 ml /16 fl oz canned
coconut milk

salt

time in kitchen 9 minutes

serves 4

total cooking time 45–55 minutes

If you do not have a traditional Moroccan earthenware tajine, use a small round flameproof casserole instead – it works perfectly. Tajines reheat well; simply refrigerate in the cooking pot for up to 2 days and reheat on the hob. Serve with couscous or boiled rice.

1 Preheat the grill. Trim the aubergines and cut them into 1 cm /½ in slices. Lay on a grill rack and sprinkle with salt and pepper. Grill about 5 cm /2 in from the heat for 5-6 minutes each side until browned.

2 Meanwhile, chop the garlic and mix together with the ginger, saffron, salt and oil in a small bowl. Arrange the chicken pieces in a single layer in the tajine or casserole. Spoon over half of the spice mixture, cover and set over a moderate heat.

3 Peel the onions, slice them and scatter over the chicken, then cover with the browned aubergine. Spoon on the remaining spice mix, cover and continue cooking on a low heat for 1 hour.

4 Test the chicken with a fork – it should be very tender. If not, cook for a further 15-30 minutes. Transfer the chicken to a warmed plate. Pour the lemon juice over the vegetables, stir well and adjust the seasoning. Replace the chicken on the vegetables and serve from the cooking pot.

Tajine of **chicken** with **aubergine**

2 medium aubergines
(about 750 g /1½ lb in total)

1 garlic clove

1 teaspoon ground ginger

large pinch of saffron powder
or threads

1 teaspoon salt, or to taste

4 tablespoons olive oil

1.8 kg /4 lb oven-ready
chicken, cut into 8 pieces

2 large onions

juice of 1 lemon

freshly ground black pepper

time in kitchen **14 minutes**   serves **4**

total cooking time 1¼–1½ hours

Cracked wheat pilaf with lamb

2 tablespoons oil

1 onion, halved and thinly sliced

250 g /8 oz lean minced lamb

300 g /10 oz coarse cracked wheat

1 tablespoon ground coriander

1 teaspoon allspice

½ teaspoon ground nutmeg

750 ml /1¼ pt veal or chicken stock or water

45 g /1½ oz dried apricots, finely chopped

75 g /2½ oz raisins

125 g /4 oz blanched pistachios

salt and freshly ground black pepper

AThe nutty flavour of cracked wheat is traditional with lamb, but for a faster cooking pilaf you can use bulgur wheat, kasha (whole buckwheat) or rice instead – follow packet directions for cooking times.

1 Heat the oil in a heavy flameproof casserole. Peel the onion, halve and thinly slice them. Add to the oil and sauté over a high heat for about 1 minute, until starting to soften.

2 Stir in the lamb and sauté for about 1 minute until the meat starts to lose its pink colour. Add the cracked wheat and cook, stirring, over a high heat for about 2 minutes.

3 Stir in the coriander, allspice and nutmeg and cook for about 30 seconds. Stir in the stock or water, apricots, raisins, pistachios, salt and pepper. Bring to the boil.

4 Cover and simmer over a low heat, without stirring, for 25-35 minutes until the liquid is absorbed. (Alternatively, microwave in a covered bowl for 10–12 minutes on high.) Taste the cracked wheat – it should be tender but still slightly chewy. If not, add a little more liquid and cook for a further 5–10 minutes (1 minute more in the microwave).

5 Leave to stand for 10 minutes, then fluff the grains with a fork and adjust the seasoning. Serve from the cooking pot.

time in kitchen **10 minutes**   serves **4**

total cooking time 30–40 minutes (15–17 using microwave)

Pork chop with a confit of onions

125 g /4 oz butter

4 pork chops (about 750 g /1½ lb in total)

6-8 Spanish onions (about 1.4 kg /3 lb)

250 ml /8 fl oz red wine

1 tablespoon sugar

salt and freshly ground pepper

Confit of onions is hard to resist, so I was determined to shorten the usual recipe to something manageable for an after-work supper. Serve with mashed potatoes or pasta.

1 Melt a quarter of the butter in a frying pan. Season the chops, add to the pan and cook over a medium heat for 4-5 minutes. Turn the chops, lower the heat and fry gently until well browned and cooked through.

2 Meanwhile, melt the remaining butter in a sauté pan or shallow casserole over a medium heat. One at a time, peel the onions, halve them, slice the halves thinly and stir into the butter.

3 When you have added 2 onions, turn the chops and lower the heat. When you have added the last onion, turn up the heat and sauté them for 2 minutes until brown and wilted.

4 Once the pork chops are cooked through, transfer them to a plate and set aside.

5 Stir the wine, sugar, salt and pepper into the onions and bring to the boil. Turn down the heat to low, press a piece of foil on top of the onions and put the lid on. Leave to simmer very gently for 30-35 minutes until meltingly soft, well browned and caramelized.

6 Lay the chops on the onions, cover tightly and warm through over a low heat for 5 minutes. Serve from the casserole or on individual plates.

time in kitchen **13 minutes**   serves **4**

total cooking time 45–50 minutes

4 garlic cloves

bunch of sage

bunch of thyme

1 teaspoon black peppercorns

3 tablespoons olive oil

1 kg /2 lb boneless rolled pork loin roast

500 ml /16 fl oz milk

salt and freshly ground black pepper

for the baker's potatoes:

2 tablespoons vegetable oil

1 large onion

4 medium potatoes (about 1 kg /2 lb)

500 ml /16 fl oz veal or chicken stock, or more if needed

Roast **pork loin** with **baker's potatoes**

Roasting pork in milk is an Italian tradition, a way to keep the pork moist and at the same time create some delectable brown gravy. Don't be put off by the curdled appearance of the gravy – it tastes wonderful.

1 Preheat the oven to 200°C/400°F/gas 6. Peel the garlic, strip the herbs from their stems and lightly crush the peppercorns. Put all of these in a food processor with 1 teaspoon salt and 2 tablespoons of the olive oil. Work to a purée.

2 Remove string and excess fat from the pork. Unroll and spread with two thirds of the herb purée (leaving the rest in the processor). Roll the pork up and tie with string.

3 Season the meat. Heat the remaining olive oil in a flameproof casserole and brown the pork over a fairly high heat, turning from time to time.

4 Meanwhile, prepare the potatoes: heat the oil in a shallow flameproof baking dish. While it is heating, peel the onion, halve it and slice it thinly. Stir into the oil and sauté the onion over a medium heat until soft. Fit the slicing blade in the processor and thinly slice the potatoes on to the remaining herb purée; toss to mix.

5 Add the potatoes to the onion, stir and spread evenly. Add the stock almost but not quite to cover the potatoes. Cover with foil and place on a low oven shelf.

6 Add the milk to the pork. Cover and place on a shelf above the potatoes. Cook both for 45-60 minutes. The potatoes should be tender and most of the stock absorbed. To test the pork, insert a skewer into the centre and leave for 30 seconds. On removing, it should be hot to the touch.

7 When the pork is cooked, set on a carving board. Boil the gravy, adjust the seasoning and pour into a serving jug. Carve the meat and serve with the gravy and potatoes.

time in kitchen **14 minutes**   serves **4**

total cooking time about 1 hour

In this recipe from Normandy, apples are combined with crème fraîche and Calvados apple brandy to make a rich sauce for baked ham. Serve with potatoes.

1 Preheat the oven to 200°C/400°F/gas 6. Melt half the butter in a frying pan over a low heat. While it heats, peel the onion, halve it and slice thinly. Stir into the butter and cook gently.

2 Quarter and core 1 apple. Thinly slice into the pan of onions. Sprinkle with 1 tablespoon of the sugar, salt and pepper and sauté briskly for 1-2 minutes until the onion and apple soften and start to brown.

3 Meanwhile, melt remaining butter in another frying pan. Core the other apple, using a corer, then cut into 1 cm /½ in rings, discarding ends. Add the apple rings to the butter, sprinkle with 1 tablespoon sugar, then turn sugar side down. Sprinkle with the remaining sugar and sauté over a medium heat for 2-3 minutes until caramelized.

4 Meanwhile, take the pan of onions off the heat, pour in the Calvados or Cognac and set alight with a match, standing back. When the flames die down, return to the heat, add the cream and bring to the boil, scraping up the sediment from the base of the pan. Season with pepper.

5 When the apple rings are caramelized, turn and brown on the other side, then remove from the heat and keep warm.

6 Cut the ham into 4 serving portions, lay in a baking dish and pour on the cream sauce. Cover with foil and bake for 15-20 minutes until bubbling. (Or microwave in a covered dish on high for 5-7 minutes.) Serve the ham on individual plates, topped with the sauce and garnished with apple rings.

Baked **ham** with **apples** & **cream**

45 g /1½ oz butter

1 onion

2 apples

30 g /1 oz sugar

3–4 tablespoons Calvados or Cognac

250 ml /8 fl oz crème fraîche or double cream

1 or 2 ham steaks, 1 cm /⅜ in thick (about 750 g /1½ lb)

salt and freshly ground black pepper

time in kitchen **8 minutes**　　　serves **4**

total cooking time 20–25 minutes (10–12 using microwave)

Jambalaya is a zesty mix of ham, vegetables, rice, chilli and plenty of prawns. Chicken or pork may also be included. For authenticity, buy a piece of smoked country ham.

1 Cut the ham into 1 cm /½ in dice. Put the oil in a large heavy casserole over a low heat, add the ham and fry gently. Halve the onion, thinly slice it and stir into the ham.

2 Halve, core and deseed the pepper. Finely dice it and stir into the ham mixture. Dice the celery and add to the casserole. Chop the garlic, stir in and cook for 1 minute.

3 Drain the juice from the tomatoes into the casserole. Roughly chop the tomatoes and add them too. Add the Worcestershire sauce, dried chilli, some black pepper and 375 ml /12 fl oz water. Stir and bring to the boil. Check the seasoning – it should be strong at this stage.

4 Stir in the prawns, then the rice. Cover the pan, lower the heat and simmer very gently for 20-25 minutes until most of the liquid is absorbed. Meanwhile, chop the parsley. If the liquid is totally absorbed before the rice is quite cooked, add half a cup of water and cook for a few minutes longer.

5 Leave the jambalaya to stand for 5-10 minutes before serving, Stir in the parsley, fluff the grains of rice with a fork and adjust the seasoning. Serve from the casserole.

Prawn Jambalaya

375 g /¾ lb thickly sliced cooked smoked ham

2 tablespoons oil

1 onion

1 green pepper

3 celery stalks

2 garlic cloves, peeled

250 g /8 oz canned tomatoes

1 tablespoon Worcestershire sauce, or to taste

½ teaspoon crushed dried red chilli pepper, or to taste

375 g /¾ lb cooked peeled medium prawns

300 g /10 oz long-grain rice

3-4 sprigs of parsley, leaves only

salt and freshly ground black pepper

time in kitchen **13 minutes**   serves **4**

total cooking time 30–35 minutes

Breton Chaudrée

1 dozen cleaned mussels

500 g /1 lb red potatoes
(unpeeled)

500 ml /16 fl oz double cream

500 ml /16 fl oz milk

250 ml /8 fl oz bottled
clam juice

1 bay leaf

30 g /1 oz butter

2 onions

500 g /1 lb cod fillets

salt and freshly ground
black pepper

This was first created by Breton fishermen who cooked up unsold or damaged fish with milk and potatoes, adding mussels for flavour. Cod is traditional, but you can use any robust white fish, or even scallops. For a full meal, serve spooned over baked *croûtes* of French bread.

1 Bring a medium pan of salted water to the boil. Cut the potatoes into 1.2 cm /½ in dice, leaving the skins on. Add the diced potato to the boiling water, cover and bring back to the boil. Simmer for 8-10 minutes, until just tender.

2 Put the cream, milk, clam juice and bay leaf in a separate pan over a low heat to warm.

3 Meanwhile, melt the butter in a large pan over a low heat. While it heats, peel the onions, halve them and slice them thinly. Stir into the butter and soften over a low heat.

4 Rinse the fish in cold water, drain and dry on kitchen paper. Cut into 2.5 cm /1 in cubes.

5 Drain the potatoes and add to the onions with some pepper. Stir in the hot cream mixture and bring just to the boil. Adjust the seasoning if necessary and simmer gently, uncovered, for 2 minutes.

6 Stir the cod into the chowder and set the mussels on top. Cover and simmer for 6-8 minutes, until the mussels open and the cod just flakes easily. Discard the bay leaf and check the seasoning. Serve at once.

time in kitchen **13 minutes**   serves **4**

total cooking time 16–20 minutes

30 g /1 oz butter

15 g /½ oz plain flour

250 ml /8 fl oz single cream

1 teaspoon dry mustard, or to taste

4 tablespoons Worcestershire sauce, or to taste

2 teaspoons Tabasco sauce, or to taste

salt and freshly ground pepper

2 eggs, plus whites of 3 more eggs

375 g /¾ lb fresh or good quality canned crab meat

Devilled crab soufflé

A hot soufflé must be served the moment it is cooked, so ensure an accompanying green salad and guests are ready. If you are in a hurry, bake it in ramekins, which take only 10-12 minutes.

1 Preheat the oven to 190°C/375°F/gas 5, positioning the oven shelf below the middle of the oven. Butter a 1.5 litre /2⅓ pt soufflé dish.

2 Melt the butter in a saucepan, add the flour and cook, stirring, until foaming. Add the cream and heat, stirring, until the sauce boils and thickens. Simmer, stirring, for 30 seconds. Off the heat, stir in the mustard, Worcestershire sauce, Tabasco, salt and pepper; set aside.

3 Separate the eggs, dropping the 2 egg yolks into the sauce and the whites into a clean bowl. Whisk the egg whites with a pinch of salt until stiff.

4 Flake the crab meat into the sauce. Stir and adjust the seasoning, adding more Tabasco, salt and pepper to taste. The mixture should be quite highly seasoned (as the egg whites will dilute the flavour).

5 Fold about a quarter of the egg whites into the crab mixture to lighten it. Add to the remaining whites and fold together as lightly as possible.

6 Transfer the mixture to the soufflé dish – it should come to within 1 cm /½ in of the rim. Smooth the top and run your thumb around the edge. (At this stage the soufflé can be refrigerated for up to 2 hours.)

7 Stand on a baking sheet and bake for 20-25 minutes, until the soufflé is puffed and brown, but still slightly soft in the centre. Serve at once.

time in kitchen **11 minutes**   serves **4**

total cooking time 25–30 minutes

This simple recipe is a perfect balance of sweet scallops, piquant shallot and fragrant '*fines herbes*' – a classic mix of chervil, tarragon and chives – moistened with butter. Serve with small boiled potatoes or some crusty bread to absorb the buttery scallop juices, and a glass of white wine.

1 Preheat the oven to 230°C/450°F/gas 8. Drain any juice from the scallops and discard the small, tough crescent-shaped membrane from the side of each one. Divide between 4 individual baking dishes or large ramekins.

2 Melt the butter in a saucepan over a low heat or in the microwave. While it is heating, peel the shallots, slice them thinly, stir into the butter and sauté to soften. (Alternatively, microwave on high for 4 minutes.)

3 Strip the chervil and tarragon leaves from the stems and chop them; snip the chives. Stir the herbs into the butter with the wine. Take off the heat and season lightly with salt and generously with pepper. Spoon the mixture over the scallops.

4 Cover the dishes with lids, or tightly with foil. Set on a baking sheet and bake for 15-20 minutes, until the scallops are just tender; do not overcook or they will be tough. (Alternatively, cover with film and microwave on high for 5-6 minutes.) Serve at once.

Baked **scallops** with **herb butter**

750 g /1½ lb shelled scallops

90 g /3 oz unsalted butter

2 shallots

small bunch of chervil

small bunch of tarragon

small bunch of chives

2 tablespoons white wine

salt and freshly ground black pepper

time in kitchen **11 minutes**   serves **4**

total cooking time 20–25 minutes (9–10 in microwave)

about 750 g /1½ lb monkfish fillets, trimmed of membrane

250 g /½ lb sliced pancetta

1 tablespoon olive oil

45 g /1½ oz butter

1 onion

1 kg /2 lb spinach

juice of ½ lemon

½ teaspoon freshly grated nutmeg

salt and freshly ground black pepper

Monkfish with pancetta & spinach

Monkfish is prized for its firm white flesh, lack of bones and sweet mild flavour. Most of it is farmed, giving fillets of a handy 375 g /¾ lb size. Here it is wrapped in Italian pancetta before baking.

1 Preheat the oven to 190°C/375°F/gas 5. Rinse the monkfish and dry on kitchen paper. Lay the pancetta slices on a work surface, overlapping them slightly. Set the monkfish fillets on top, head to tail, to form a cylinder. Wrap the pancetta around them or, if necessary, cover with another layer of pancetta and secure with string.

2 Brush a roasting pan with the oil. Season the fish, place in the pan and bake for 25-30 minutes. (Alternatively microwave in a suitable dish, covered tightly with microwave film, on high for 15-18 minutes.)

3 Meanwhile, heat the butter in a sauté pan or deep frying pan. While it is heating, peel the onion, halve and thinly slice, stir into the butter and sauté over medium heat until soft. Remove the stems from the spinach and add with some seasoning. Toss over the heat for 1-2 minutes until wilted. Add the lemon juice and nutmeg, check the seasoning and set aside.

4 To test the roast, insert a skewer into the centre of the fish and leave for 30 seconds. On removing, it should feel hot. When cooked, transfer to a carving board. Put the spinach in the roasting pan, stir and reheat in the oven. (Allow 45-60 seconds on high in the microwave.)

5 Meanwhile, carve the roast into thick slices. Arrange on a warmed platter or individual plates with the spinach.

time in kitchen **11 minutes**   serves **4**

total cooking time 25–30 minutes (15–18 in microwave)

Buy thick fillets of a robust fish, such as red snapper, cod or halibut for this dish. After baking with the tapenade, the fish becomes deliciously perfumed with olives. Serve with Provençal Tricolor (page 101), or roasted sweet peppers.

1 Preheat the oven to 190°C/375°F/gas 5. Put the bread in a bowl, pour on 125 ml /4 fl oz cold water and leave to soak.

2 Brush a baking dish with olive oil. Rinse and dry the fish, cut into 4 pieces and lay in the dish. Cut 4 slices from the lemon; squeeze the juice from the rest and set aside.

3 For the tapenade, peel the garlic and put it in a food processor with the olives, anchovies, drained and rinsed capers and almonds. Squeeze out excess water from the bread, then add to the processor. Pulse to coarsely chop the ingredients. With the motor running, gradually add the oil and process until smooth. Add lemon juice and plenty of pepper, to taste.

4 Spoon some tapenade on to each piece of fish and top with a lemon slice. Bake for 12-15 minutes, until the fish just flakes easily. (Alternatively, microwave in a suitable dish covered with microwave film on high for 5-6 minutes.) Serve from the baking dish.

Snapper with green olive tapenade

olive oil, for brushing

500 g /1 lb red snapper fillets

1 lemon

for the tapenade:

1 slice of white bread

2 garlic cloves

75 g /2½ oz pitted green olives

2 anchovy fillets

2 tablespoons capers

30 g /1 oz flaked almonds

4 tablespoons olive oil

freshly ground black pepper

time in kitchen **10 minutes**   serves **4**

total cooking time 12–15 minutes (6 in microwave)

Roast fish belle florence

4 tablespoons olive oil

1 onion

500 g /1 lb tomatoes

250 g /½ lb mushrooms

1 tablespoon dried mixed Provençal herbs

1 whole fish (see right), weighing about 1.5 kg /3½ lb, cleaned, scaled and trimmed

1 lemon

4 sprigs of fresh thyme

salt and pepper

Salmon, bream and sea bass are particularly good for roasting, but don't overlook more modest hake or trout. For speed I suggest one large fish to serve 4, roasting it for 30-35 minutes. Or you can substitute two smaller fish, each about 750 g /1½ lb, roasting them for 25-30 minutes.

1 Preheat the oven to 190°C/375°F/gas 5. Heat half the oil in a flameproof roasting pan (large enough to take the fish). While it is heating, peel the onion, halve, slice thinly and stir into the oil. Sauté over medium heat to soften.

2 Core the tomatoes and slice them thickly. Trim off the stems from the mushrooms, wipe the caps and slice them thickly. Add the tomatoes, mushrooms, dried herbs, salt and pepper to the onions. Stir to mix and leave to cook over medium heat.

3 Meanwhile, rinse the fish inside and out; pat dry with kitchen paper. Diagonally slash each side of the fish in 4 places. Cut 2 slices from the lemon; halve these. Insert a thyme sprig and a lemon slice in each slash on the upper side of the fish.

4 Take the roasting pan off the heat and lay the fish on the vegetables. Squeeze the juice from the rest of the lemon over the fish and drizzle with the remaining olive oil. Season with salt and pepper.

5 Cover the roasting pan with foil and bake for 30-35 minutes, until the fish flakes when tested with a fork and is opaque in the centre. Transfer to a serving platter. Check the seasoning of the vegetables and spoon around the fish. Serve hot, or at room temperature.

time in kitchen **12 minutes**   serves **4**

total cooking time 40–45 minutes

2 medium fennel bulbs

75 g /2½ oz butter

4 trout fillets (each about 175 g /6 oz)

1 medium bunch of dill

4 tablespoons Pernod or other aniseed-flavoured liquor

salt and freshly ground black pepper

Trout with fennel & herbs en papillote

Fish is particularly suited to cooking 'en papillote' whether it's salmon, sea bass or trout as suggested here. All the juices are retained inside the parcels and the aroma when a papillote is broken open at the table is half of its charm.

1 Preheat the oven to 190°C/375°F/gas 5. Halve and thinly slice the fennel. Melt half the butter in a frying pan. Add the fennel with salt and pepper to taste and press a piece of foil on top. Cook over a high heat for 3-4 minutes, stirring occasionally, until the fennel is slightly softened.

2 Meanwhile, melt the remaining butter in a small pan or in the microwave. Cut 4 sheets of greaseproof paper, each about 30 x 40 cm /12 x 16 in. Fold each in half lengthwise, then open them out again and brush with melted butter.

3 Rinse the trout fillets and dry on kitchen paper. Set aside 4 dill sprigs. Strip the leaves from the rest, chop coarsely, then stir into the fennel. Check the seasoning.

4 Arrange a bed of fennel on one side of each piece of paper, and lay a trout fillet on top. Sprinkle with salt, pepper and Pernod and top with a dill sprig. Fold the paper over the trout to enclose and press the edges together. Starting at one side of the fold, pleat the paper on itself to seal the edges, working around to finish again at the fold.

5 Transfer the parcels to a baking sheet and bake for 25-35 minutes until puffed and brown. Transfer to warmed plates and serve at once, allowing guests to open their own parcel.

time in kitchen 14 minutes   **serves 4**

total cooking time 30–40 minutes

Chapter 3

15 minutes

to table

It's surprising what can be cooked in 15 minutes, with a little imagination and a compliant main ingredient, such as fish, minute steak or veal escalope. For a simple satisfying meal, pasta must come near the top of the list. Try Bow-ties with Wild Mushrooms & Nuts, or Oriental-style Stir-fried Rice Noodles with Prawns.

Even when you've had no time to shop, if you follow the advice in The Well-stocked Store-cupboard (page 8) you can fall back on eggs, pasta or a quickly simmered vegetable soup. It pays to keep on hand items such as olive oil, wine vinegar and Parmesan, not to mention wine, garlic, spring onions and a herb or two.

I hope you'll use these recipes as a starting point, inventing your variations. For instance, you can fill the Open-faced Omelette with almost anything you have on hand, from cooked chicken or fish to vegetables and cheese. Both Stir-fried Rice Noodles with Prawns and Spiced Indonesian Stir-fry are equally accommodating.

Team any of the recipes in this section with something from Speedy Salads, such as Wilted Frisée with Bacon Salad, Panzanella or Crazy Salad, all of which take less than 15 minutes. Add a quick idea from Fast finishes, like Strawberry Burnt Cream or Orange Salad with Caramel and you have a three-course menu ready in less than an hour.

Fifteen-minute minestrone

1 bay leaf

1 leek

3 celery stalks

2 tablespoons olive oil

175 g /6 oz slice of country ham

1 garlic clove

2 small courgettes

50 g /1½ oz pasta bows

250 g /8 oz can of plum tomatoes

250 g /8 oz can of white kidney beans

salt and freshly ground black pepper

4 sprigs of flat-leaf parsley, to garnish

60 g /2 oz Parmesan cheese, grated, to serve

Omit slow-cooking vegetables like carrot and fennel, use canned tomatoes and kidney beans, and you'll be surprised what a satisfying soup can be simmered in such a short time. Serve it at once to capture the burst of vegetable flavours – with Italian bread for a complete meal.

1 Bring 1 litre /1⅔ pt of water to the boil with the bay leaf in a large covered soup pot.

2 Trim and thinly slice the leek and celery. Heat the oil in a frying pan. Add the celery, leek and some pepper, cover with foil and cook gently to soften. Trim any fat from the ham and dice the ham. Peel the garlic and chop it. Add these to the vegetables, replacing the foil.

3 Quarter the courgettes lengthwise, then slice. Drop into the pan of boiling water with some pepper. Add the pasta, re-cover and bring back to the boil.

4 Drain the juice from the tomatoes into the soup. Coarsely chop the tomatoes and add them too. Stir in the beans with their liquid, then the vegetables and ham. Bring to the boil and simmer for 3-4 minutes. Discard the bay leaf.

5 Check the seasoning. Spoon into bowls and top with parsley sprigs. Serve the Parmesan separately.

time in kitchen **15 minutes**   serves **4**

total cooking time 15 minutes

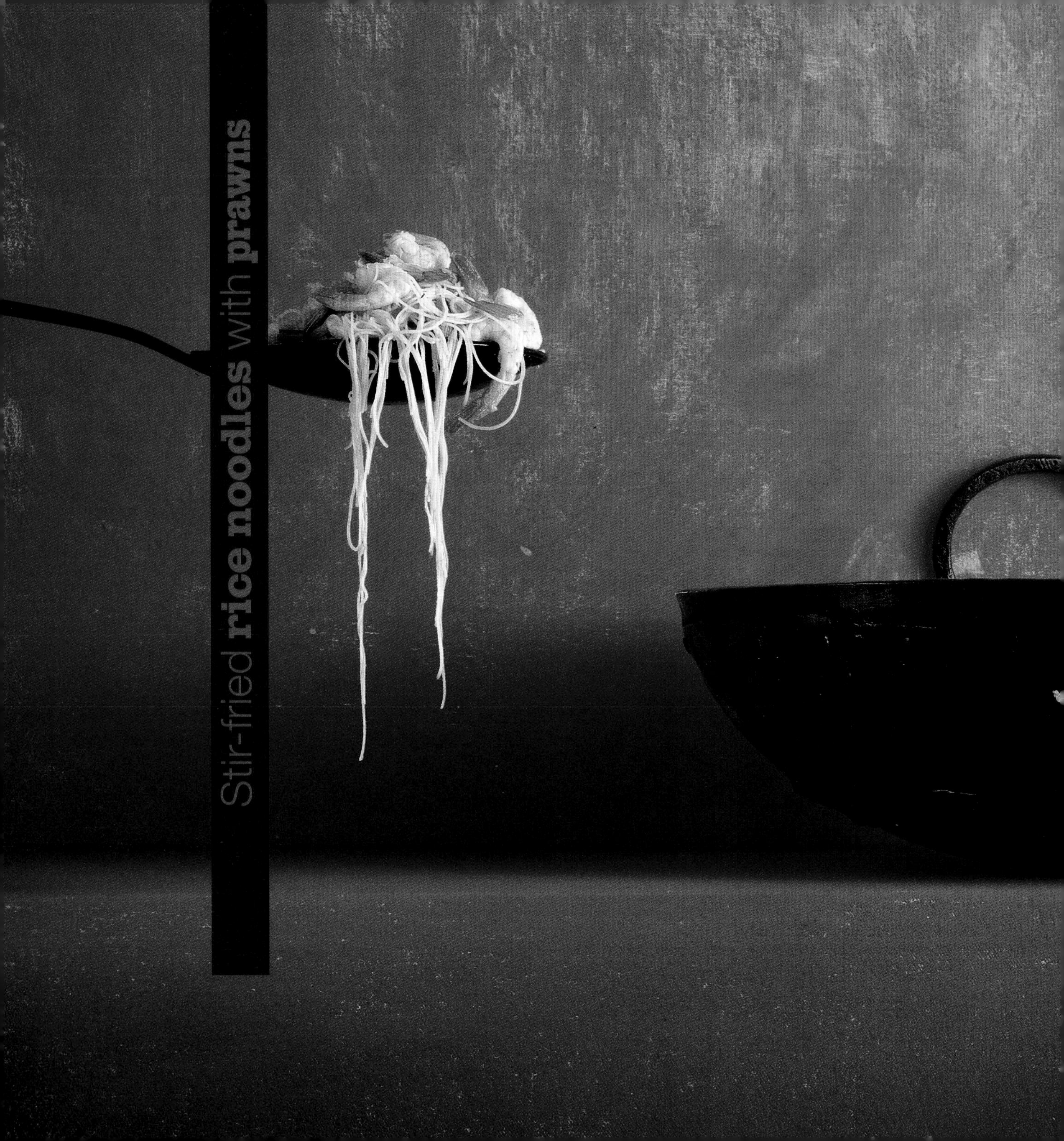

Stir-fried **rice noodles** with **prawns**

5-7 spring onions

2 garlic cloves

2.5 cm /1 in piece of fresh ginger

3 tablespoons soy sauce, or to taste

1 teaspoon Chinese red chilli paste, or to taste

375 g /¾ lb thin rice noodles

4 tablespoons vegetable oil

375 g /¾ lb small peeled cooked prawns

1 teaspoon sesame oil, or to taste

I was introduced to the wok after many years of using only French kitchen equipment and became an instant fan. The fast heat transfer makes stir-frying one of the quickest of techniques.

1 Bring a covered medium pan of salted water to the boil. Slice the green part of the spring onions diagonally.

2 Peel the garlic cloves. Trim the spring onions and slice the green parts at an angle. Cut the ginger into smallish chunks.

3 Put the white part of the spring onions in a food processor with the garlic and ginger. Pulse for 15-30 seconds to chop. Combine the soy sauce and chilli paste in a small bowl.

4 Add the noodles to the boiling water, stir and simmer for 1-2 minutes, until they are tender but still chewy.

5 Meanwhile, heat the vegetable oil in the wok for about 10 seconds, just until it starts to smoke. Immediately add the garlic, ginger and spring onion mixture with the prawns and stir-fry for 1 minute. Take off the heat.

6 Drain the cooked noodles, add to the wok and return to the heat. Toss for 1-2 minutes, until the prawns and noodles are very hot.

7 Add the soy sauce and chilli paste and stir-fry for 20-30 seconds. Add the spring onion tops and sprinkle with the sesame oil. Stir and taste, adding more soy, chilli paste and sesame oil if you wish. Serve at once.

Stir-fried **rice noodles** with **black mushrooms**

Replace the prawns with 15 g /½ oz dried black Chinese mushrooms, soaked in boiling water, drained and sliced. Add a small handful of chopped coriander leaves to serve.

time in kitchen **10 minutes**　serves **4**

total cooking time 4 minutes

375 g /¾ lb smoked
haddock fillets

250 ml /8 fl oz milk

8 eggs

60 g /2 oz Parmesan cheese,
grated

30 g /1 oz butter

125 ml /4 fl oz double cream

salt and freshly ground
black pepper

Open-faced omelette of smoked haddock

An open-faced omelette requires no tricky folding or flipping. All sorts of flavourings are possible – smoked salmon or mackerel can replace the smoked haddock used here. Serve with a green salad and a crusty baguette.

1 Preheat the grill. Lay the haddock, skin side up, in a saucepan. Add the milk, cover and simmer for 2-3 minutes until the fish flakes easily.

2 Meanwhile, whisk the eggs in a bowl with some pepper for about 30 seconds, until frothy.

3 Drain the fish and place, skin side up, on a cold plate. Peel off the skin and flake the flesh, removing any residual bones. Stir the fish and half of the cheese into the eggs.

4 Heat the butter in a 30 cm /12 in omelette pan or frying pan until it just starts to brown. Add the egg mixture and stir briskly with a fork for 20-30 seconds, until the eggs start to cook and thicken.

5 Pull the cooked edges from the side to the centre, tipping the pan so the uncooked egg runs to the side. Continue until the egg is lightly set on the bottom but still soft on top. Cook for about 30 seconds without stirring to brown the base. Remove from the heat.

6 Pour on the cream and sprinkle with the remaining cheese. Put the omelette under the grill for 1-2 minutes until brown. Serve at once, cut into wedges.

time in kitchen **10 minutes**   serves **4**

total cooking time 6–8 minutes

The culinary term 'marchand de vin' denotes pan-frying a juicy beef steak with a finishing touch of red wine, shallots and herbs. Here tuna, the 'steak' of today, is given the same treatment – delicious! Swordfish is an alternative to tuna, and chives, chervil or dill can replace tarragon.

1 Cut the butter into cubes and heat a quarter of it in a heavy frying pan until foaming. Season the tuna steaks with salt and pepper, add to the pan and sauté over a fairly high heat for about 2 minutes. Meanwhile, peel the shallots and slice them thinly.

2 Turn the tuna steaks and cook for a further 1-2 minutes according to taste. Meanwhile, strip the herbs from the stems and chop the tarragon and parsley leaves together. Transfer the tuna steaks to a warmed plate, cover and keep warm.

3 To make the sauce, add the shallots to the frying pan and sauté for 1-2 minutes. Add the wine and boil rapidly until reduced by half. Take off the heat and whisk in the remaining butter until it softens and thickens the sauce slightly. Stir in the herbs and adjust the seasoning.

4 Set the tuna steaks on 4 warmed plates, spoon over the sauce and serve at once.

60 g /2 oz cold unsalted butter

4 tuna steaks (about 625 g /1¼ lb in total)

2 shallots

small bunch of tarragon

2-3 parsley sprigs

250 ml /8 fl oz red wine

salt and freshly ground black pepper

Tuna steak marchand de vin

time in kitchen **10 minutes**   serves **4**
total cooking time 6–8 minutes

Swordfish must be cooked quickly or it becomes dry. Here it is seared on the outside while remaining juicy inside. Tuna steaks are an alternative. Serve a colourful accompaniment, such as fresh green tagliatelle, broccoli or sugar snap peas.

1 Preheat the grill. Boil the wine for the sauce in a heavy-based pan until reduced to about 1 tablespoon; this will take 3-4 minutes.

2 Cut the butter into pieces. Lay the swordfish steaks on the rack in the foil-lined grill pan and dot with the butter. Grill for 5-6 minutes about 7.5 cm /3 in from the heat; there's no need to turn the steaks.

3 Meanwhile, add the cream and saffron to the reduced wine and boil again until reduced to about 3 tablespoons. Take off the heat, cut the butter for the sauce into cubes and add a few at a time, whisking vigorously and moving the pan on and off the heat so the butter emulsifies without turning oily; this will take 2-3 minutes. Adjust the seasoning; the flavour should be delicate. Set aside.

4 When the fish is lightly browned, test the centre of one steak with the point of a knife – a thin translucent layer should remain in the middle. Transfer the steaks to warmed plates and spoon over a little of the saffron sauce; serve the rest separately.

Grilled **swordfish** with **saffron butter**

30 g /1 oz butter

4 swordfish steaks, 2 cm / ¾ in thick (about 625 g /1¼ lb)

salt and freshly ground black pepper

for the saffron butter sauce:

3½ tablespoons white wine

5 tablespoons double cream

large pinch of saffron threads

175 g /6 oz cold unsalted butter

time in kitchen **9 minutes**   serves **4**

total cooking time 7–9 minutes

Fried **mackerel** in **oatmeal**

60 g /2 oz flour

½ teaspoon pepper

1 teaspoon salt

2 eggs

3 tablespoons Dijon-style mustard

200 g /6½ oz rolled oats

8 skinless mackerel fillets (about 625 g /1¼ lb in total)

5 tablespoons vegetable oil

lemon wedges, to serve

Mackerel fillets are coated in mustard and oatmeal, which fries to a crunchy, tasty crust. Serve with fried tomatoes or a simple salad of sliced tomatoes.

1 Put the flour on a deep plate and season with the pepper and half the salt. Break the eggs on to a second plate, add the mustard and remaining salt and whisk with a fork until well mixed. Spread the rolled oats on a third plate.

2 Rinse the fish fillets and dry on kitchen paper. Dip one fillet into the flour to coat thoroughly, then lift out and pat the coating evenly. Holding it by the tail, dip in the egg and brush to coat both sides. Finally coat with the oats, pressing them on with your hand. Transfer to a tray. Repeat with the remaining fillets.

3 Heat the oil in a large frying pan until very hot. Add half the fish fillets and fry over a high heat for about 2 minutes on each side until golden. Drain on kitchen paper while frying the remainder. Serve at once, garnished with lemon wedges.

Cajun **catfish** in **cornmeal**

Use catfish or herring instead of mackerel. Omit the mustard. Add 1 tablespoon of Cajun Fish Spice (a mix of chilli, paprika, cayenne and allspice) to the flour, more if you like it spicier. Substitute coarse-ground yellow cornmeal or polenta for the rolled oats.

time in kitchen **12 minutes**   serves **4**

total cooking time 5 minutes

time in kitchen **14 minutes**

total cooking time 12–14 minutes

serves **4**

Kedgeree is a striking golden mix of rice and smoked fish, aromatic with curry spices and green with fresh herbs. The traditional fish to use is smoked haddock, but kippers and salmon are acceptable alternatives.

1 Bring a large pan of salted water to the boil, then add the rice, stir and simmer for 10-12 minutes, stirring once or twice during cooking to prevent sticking.

2 Heat the milk in a pan. Cut the fish into 2 or 3 pieces, then place skin side up in the pan. Bring to a simmer and cook for 2-3 minutes, until the fish flakes easily.

3 Melt a third of the butter in a frying pan. While it is heating, peel the onion, slice it thinly and stir it into the butter. Sauté over a medium heat for 1-2 minutes.

Kedgeree

300 g /10 oz long-grain
white rice

500 ml /16 fl oz milk

750 g /1½ lb smoked
haddock fillets

45 g /1½ oz butter

1 onion

small bunch of fresh coriander
or parsley

1 tablespoon curry powder

125 ml /4 fl oz double cream

salt and freshly ground
black pepper

pinch of cayenne pepper
(optional)

4 When the fish is cooked, drain and transfer to a plate; let cool slightly. Remove the skin and flake the fish, discarding any bones. Strip the coriander or parsley leaves from the stems and chop the leaves.

5 When cooked, drain the rice in a colander and rinse with hot water. Clean the pan, then melt the remaining butter in it. Add the rice and keep warm over a very low heat.

6 Stir the curry powder into the onion and sauté for about 1 minute. Add the fish and cream and heat through, stirring, for about 1 minute. Add to the rice with the herbs and toss over a high heat until fragrant and very hot.

7 Check the seasoning, adding a pinch of cayenne if you wish. Serve in a large bowl or on individual plates.

1 carrot

1 large fillet of salmon with skin (about 625 g /1¼ lb)

knob of butter

250 ml /8 fl oz double cream

small bunch of tarragon

2 teaspoons Dijon mustard, or to taste

salt and freshly ground black pepper

Salmon escalopes with mustard sauce

Thin salmon escalopes are served with a creamy sauce, flavoured with mustard and tarragon. Try using a different mustard – perhaps one with seeds, or flavoured with orange. Monkfish can be used instead of salmon.

1 Bring a small pan of salted water to the boil. Cut the carrot into thin julienne strips, add to the boiling water and simmer for 4-5 minutes, until just tender; drain.

2 Meanwhile, cut the salmon fillet diagonally into at least 8 escalopes, about 1 cm /½ in thick, off the skin. Sprinkle with salt and pepper.

3 Preheat a non-stick frying pan, then brush with a little butter. Add half of the salmon and cook over a high heat for 30-60 seconds on each side – the escalopes should still be slightly translucent in the centre. Transfer to a warm plate and keep warm while cooking the rest of the salmon. Remove these and keep warm.

4 Add the cream to the pan and bring to the boil. In the meantime, strip the tarragon leaves from the stems and coarsely chop the leaves. Whisk the mustard into the cream – it will emulsify and thicken the sauce slightly. Stir in the chopped tarragon, carrot julienne and seasoning to taste.

5 Transfer the salmon to 4 warmed plates and spoon on the sauce to serve.

time in kitchen **10 minutes**   serves **4**

total cooking time 6–8 minutes

Buy fresh tagliatelle from an Italian deli or supermarket, or use dried pasta. Scallops or prawns can replace sole, and tarragon, chives or parsley can be used instead of basil.

1 Bring a large covered pan of salted water to the boil. Rinse the sole fillets and dry on kitchen paper towel. Cut each one diagonally into 3 or 4 strips.

2 Melt half the butter in a large frying pan and add the sole strips. Pour on the wine, season the fish and cook for 1 minute, stirring once or twice, until the strips are firm and white on the outside. Transfer to a plate.

3 Add the cream to the pan, stir and simmer for 1-2 minutes, until reduced by half. Core, halve, deseed and finely chop the tomatoes. Add to the reducing cream.

4 Meanwhile, cook the tagliatelle in the boiling water for 1-2 minutes, stirring occasionally, until al dente – tender but firm to the bite. Coarsely shred the basil leaves, reserving a few for garnish. Take the sauce from the heat.

5 Drain the tagliatelle in a colander. Melt the remaining butter in the pan, add the tagliatelle with some pepper and toss until coated with butter. Transfer to a large warm serving bowl and make a hollow in the centre.

6 Bring the sauce just back to the boil. Add the sole with any juices, and chopped basil. Heat through gently, stirring carefully; do not overcook. Adjust the seasoning. Add to the pasta, top with basil leaves and serve at once.

Tagliatelle with sole & basil

500 g /1 lb sole fillets

60 g /2 oz butter

175 ml /6 fl oz dry white wine

375 ml /12 fl oz double cream

3 plum tomatoes

500 g /1 lb fresh green tagliatelle

large bunch of basil, leaves only

salt and freshly ground black pepper

time in kitchen **10 minutes**   serves **4**

total cooking time 3–4 minutes

Tagliatelle with coriander & ginger

Coriander forms a brisk trio with lime and fresh ginger in this recipe, which could hardly be quicker to assemble. Smoked salmon is the perfect complement.

1 Bring a large covered pan of salted water to the boil. Finely chop the ginger. Strip the coriander leaves from the stems and coarsely chop them.

2 Cook the tagliatelle in the boiling water for 1-2 minutes, stirring occasionally, until al dente – tender but firm to the bite. Meanwhile, grate the zest from the limes and squeeze the juice from one of them.

3 Drain the pasta in a colander. Wipe out the pan, then heat the olive oil in it. Add the ginger and sauté for about 1 minute, until fragrant. Add the tagliatelle with the coriander and lime zest and toss over the heat for about 1 minute, until the pasta is very hot and coated with oil.

4 Add the lime juice, white pepper and a little salt, toss well and check the seasoning. Pile the tagliatelle on to 4 warmed plates. Add a slice of smoked salmon to each and serve at once.

5 cm/2 in piece of fresh ginger

large bunch of fresh coriander (about 60 g /2 oz)

500 g /1 lb fresh tagliatelle

2 limes

5 tablespoons olive oil

½ teaspoon ground white pepper, or to taste

4 slices of smoked salmon (about 175 g /6 oz)

salt

time in kitchen **14 minutes**   serves **4**

total cooking time 3–4 minutes

Piquant steak with tomato

2 spring onions

3-4 parsley sprigs

1 large tomato

1 tablespoon oil

15 g /½ oz butter

8 minute steaks (about 750 g /1½ lb), pounded flat

3 tablespoons Cognac

1 tablespoon Worcestershire sauce

250 ml /8 fl oz beef or veal stock

salt and freshly ground black pepper

Tender minute steaks, cut from the thin tail end of the fillet, are ideal for this recipe. Allow two per person and ask your butcher to pound them flat.

1 Bring a small, deep covered pan of water to the boil. In the meantime, thinly slice the spring onions at an angle. Strip the parsley leaves from the stems and chop the leaves.

2 Scoop out the core of the tomato, then immerse in the boiling water for 10-15 seconds to loosen the skin. Drain, cool under cold running water, then peel. Halve, deseed and chop the tomato.

3 Heat the oil and butter in a frying pan until foaming. Season the steaks and fry half of them in the pan over a high heat for 30-60 seconds on each side until browned, but still rare in the centre. Transfer to a warmed plate; keep warm while frying the rest. Move to the warm plate.

4 Pour off any excess fat from the pan then, off the heat, add the Cognac and set alight with a match, standing well back. Return to the heat.

5 When the flames die down, add the spring onions to the pan and cook for 30 seconds, until slightly soft. Stir in the tomato, Worcestershire sauce, stock and seasoning, and bring to the boil. Replace the steaks, baste with the sauce and heat through for 1 minute.

6 Transfer steaks to 4 warmed plates. Stir the parsley into the sauce, adjust seasoning and simmer briefly to thicken if necessary. Spoon over the steaks and serve at once.

time in kitchen **9 minutes**   serves **4**

total cooking time 3–4 minutes

For this simplified Mongolian Hot-pot, a pot of boiling flavoured water is placed on a sturdy stand over a burner in the centre of the table. Each guest dips slivers of raw beef, scallops, bean curd and vegetables into the pot with chopsticks. Finally, noodles are simmered in the aromatic broth, which is served as a soup to round off the meal.

1 Bring 2 litres /3¼ pt of water to the boil with the salt and ginger added.

2 Meanwhile, arrange the beef slices on one side of 4 large plates. Pat the scallops dry, discard the crescent-shaped membrane and halve horizontally if large. Arrange on the plates. Cut the tofu into large cubes and add. Remove the stems from the spinach. Trim the bok-choy and cut into 2.5 cm /1 in slices. Trim the spring onions. Arrange the vegetables on the plates.

3 Chop the coriander and put in a small bowl.

4 For the sauce, stir the tahini paste, soy sauce, chilli paste or Tabasco, and vinegar together in a bowl until smooth. Stir in 4 tablespoons of water. Adjust the flavouring to taste and spoon into 4 small dipping bowls.

5 Transfer the pot – which should now be boiling – to the table burner. Adjust the heat so the liquid simmers. Set the plates of meat and vegetables at each place, with chopsticks and a bowl of sauce. Invite guests to cook their ingredients in the pot, then dip into the sauce before eating.

6 Towards the end of the meal, add the rice noodles and coriander to the pot with any remaining raw ingredients and bring the soup back to the boil. (If necessary, return to the hob to bring to a full boil.) Simmer for 1 minute, until the noodles are just tender, then serve in warmed bowls.

Fifteen-minute fire pot

500 g /1 lb raw beef fillet, cut into wafer-thin slices across the grain

125 g /4 oz scallops

125 g /4 oz tofu

250 g /½ lb baby spinach

1 small head of bok-choy (about 375 g /¾ lb)

4 spring onions

small bunch of fresh coriander

45 g /1½ oz medium rice noodles

for the pot:

1 tablespoon salt

2.5 cm/1 in piece of ginger, sliced

for the sauce:

125 g /4 oz tahini paste

2 teaspoons dark soy sauce

2 teaspoons red chilli paste or a few drops Tabasco sauce

4 teaspoons rice or red wine vinegar

time in kitchen **15 minutes**   serves **4**

Veal piccatine with mushrooms & marsala

4 veal escalopes (about 500 g /1 lb)

60 g /2 oz plain flour

1 teaspoon salt, or to taste

½ teaspoon pepper, or to taste

125 g /4 oz mushrooms

60 g /2 oz butter

125 ml /4 fl oz dry Marsala

125 ml /4 fl oz double cream

'*Piccatine*' is the Venetian name for tiny veal escalopes, thinly cut from larger ones and served 3 to 4 per person. Buy veal which is moist, light pink and fine-textured.

1 Pound the veal escalopes between two sheets of plastic film on a board to flatten slightly, then cut each one into 3 or 4 pieces. Put the flour on a plate and season with the salt and pepper. Trim off the mushroom stems, wipe the caps and slice them thinly.

2 Heat half the butter in a large frying pan over a fairly high heat and cook the piccatine in 3 or 4 batches. Dip in the flour, pat to coat both sides, then add to the pan in a single layer. Fry briskly for 30-60 seconds on each side until brown. (Meanwhile, coat the other piccatine). Transfer to a warmed plate and fry the remaining piccatine, adding a little more butter if needed. Transfer to the plate.

3 Melt the remaining butter in the pan and add the mushrooms. Season and cook, stirring, for about 2 minutes until tender and almost all their liquid has evaporated.

4 Add the Marsala and simmer, stirring, until reduced by about half. Stir in the cream and bring to the boil. Add the piccatine to the sauce and heat through gently for about 1 minute. Check the seasoning of the sauce.

5 Transfer the piccatine to warmed plates and spoon on the mushrooms and sauce to serve.

time in kitchen **11 minutes**   serves **4**

total cooking time 7–9 minutes

Spiced indonesian **stir-fry**

2 garlic cloves

½ teaspoon crushed dried red chilli pepper

2 teaspoons ground coriander

2 teaspoons ground ginger

3 tablespoons dark soy sauce

3 tablespoons rice vinegar

750 g /1½ lb boneless chicken breast, or 2 cm / ¾ in thick fillet steaks, or boned pork loin

2 tablespoons groundnut or vegetable oil

for the cucumber salad:

1 large cucumber

small bunch of fresh coriander, leaves only

250 ml /8 fl oz plain yogurt

salt and freshly ground black pepper

This recipe is versatile, as tender cuts of chicken, pork and beef marry well with the same zesty spice mix. Serve with boiled rice, as well as the cucumber salad.

1 For the salad, peel, halve and deseed the cucumber, then slice thinly and place in a bowl. Coarsely chop the coriander and add two thirds to the cucumber. Mix in the yogurt and salt and pepper to taste; set aside.

2 Peel the garlic and chop it finely. Mix the garlic, chilli, ground coriander, ginger, soy sauce and vinegar together in a bowl; set aside.

3 If using chicken, remove any skin, then cut into 2.5 cm / 1 in cubes. If using beef or pork, trim off any fat or sinew, then cut into 2 cm /¾ in cubes.

4 Heat the oil in the wok until almost smoking. Add the chicken or meat and cook, stirring, over a high heat for about 2 minutes, until lightly browned. Add the spice mix and stir-fry for 30-60 seconds longer: chicken and pork should be well done; beef should be rare in the centre.

5 Scatter over the reserved coriander. Serve at once accompanied by the cucumber salad and boiled rice.

time in kitchen **12 minutes**   serves **4**

total cooking time 3–4 minutes

500 g /1 lb spaghetti

75 g /2½ oz pitted olives in oil

60 g /2 oz sun-dried tomatoes in oil

45 g /1½ oz capers

3 garlic cloves

½ teaspoon dried red pepper flakes, or to taste

4 tablespoons olive oil

small bunch of flat-leaf parsley

salt and freshly ground black pepper

Sicilian spaghetti

This pungent sauce is reminiscent of the famous '*spaghetti alla puttanesca*'. Sun-dried tomatoes replace the usual fresh tomatoes and anchovies, and the sauce is puréed. It keeps well in a covered jar, for at least a week in the refrigerator.

1 Bring a large covered pan of salted water to the boil. Cook the spaghetti in the boiling water for 8-10 minutes, stirring occasionally, until al dente – tender but firm to the bite.

2 Meanwhile, set aside a quarter of the olives, sun-dried tomatoes and drained capers. Peel the garlic cloves and put in a food processor with the remaining three-quarters of each and the red pepper flakes. Work in all but 1 tablespoon of the olive oil, to a smooth purée.

3 Shred the reserved sun-dried tomatoes. Strip the parsley leaves from the stems and chop the leaves, reserving a few sprigs for garnish.

4 Drain the cooked spaghetti in a colander. Add the reserved olive oil to the pan, then return the pasta and add the sauce and chopped parsley. Toss until the spaghetti is well coated. Adjust the seasoning.

5 Pile the spaghetti into a warmed serving bowl. Sprinkle with the reserved olives, capers and sun-dried tomato. Garnish with parsley and serve at once.

time in kitchen **12 minutes**   serves **4**

total cooking time 8–10 minutes

For this simple recipe, olive oil is heated, then poured over sage leaves to develop their full flavour and aroma. Basil, oregano or flat-leaf parsley can be used instead of the sage.

1 Bring a large covered pan of salted water to the boil. Cook the spaghetti in the boiling water for 8-10 minutes, stirring occasionally, until al dente – tender but firm to the bite.

2 Meanwhile, pull the sage leaves from the stems, coarsely shred them and put them in a large serving bowl. Heat the oil gently in a small pan.

3 Drain the cooked spaghetti in a colander. When the oil is aromatic and almost starting to smoke, pour it over the sage leaves – they should sizzle slightly. Add the drained spaghetti and toss vigorously.

4 Serve at once, with grated Parmesan cheese.

Tagliatelle with parsley & pine nuts

Substitute coarsely chopped flat-leaf parsley for the sage. Cook the tagliatelle. Heat 1 tablespoon of the oil in a small frying pan and sauté 60 g /2 oz pine nuts for 1-2 minutes until brown. Add to the parsley. Heat the remaining oil and continue as above. Sprinkle with 1 tablespoon of balsamic vinegar to serve.

Emma's spaghetti with sage

500 g /1 lb spaghetti

2 large bunches of sage

125 ml /4 fl oz olive oil

salt and freshly ground black pepper

grated Parmesan cheese, to serve

time in kitchen **12 minutes**

total cooking time 8–10 minutes

serves **4**

Bow-ties with wild mushrooms & nuts

125 g /4 oz skinned hazelnuts

60 g /2 oz dried mushrooms, such as shiitake

500 g /1 lb dried bow-tie pasta

250 g /½ lb fresh wild mushrooms, such as shiitake or chanterelles

2 garlic cloves

45 g /1½ oz butter

125 ml /4 fl oz white wine

250 ml /8 fl oz double cream

salt and freshly ground black pepper

Dried mushrooms add intensity and toasted hazelnuts highlight the earthy flavour of the wild mushrooms.

1 Preheat the oven to 200°C/400°F/gas 6. Bring a large covered pan of salted water to the boil. Toast the hazelnuts on a baking sheet in the oven for 8-10 minutes.

2 Put the dried mushrooms in a small bowl and add enough boiling water to cover.

3 Meanwhile, cook the pasta in the boiling water for 8-10 minutes, stirring occasionally, until al dente – tender but firm to the bite.

4 While the pasta is cooking, trim off the fresh mushroom stems, brush the caps and cut them into large pieces. Peel the garlic cloves and chop them.

5 Melt the butter in a large frying pan, then add the fresh mushrooms, garlic and seasoning. Sauté over a high heat, while preparing the dried mushrooms. Drain these, trim and cut into pieces. Stir into the fresh mushrooms with the wine. Simmer for 2-3 minutes, until most of the liquid has evaporated. Meanwhile, coarsely crush the toasted nuts.

6 Drain the cooked pasta and return to the pan. Stir the cream into the mushrooms and bring to the boil. Adjust the seasoning.

7 Pour the mushroom sauce over the pasta, add the hazelnuts and toss over a medium heat for 30-60 seconds until hot. Check the seasoning. Serve on warmed plates.

time in kitchen **13 minutes**   serves **4**

total cooking time 12 minutes

speedy

salads

Because they involve preparing a multiplicity of vegetables, many salads are not speedy at all. So we focus on recipes with at most three or four main ingredients, such as the Wilted Frisée & Bacon Salad or Panzanella. Using ham, prawns or other meats and fish which come ready-cooked is also time-saving. The pungency of cheese is a boon, as is the saltiness of anchovy and olives, and the zest of spring onions and garlic.

Next, beware of any single ingredient that takes a long time to prepare – even a head of lettuce takes about 3 minutes to trim, wash and dry thoroughly. Greens which need little more than a rinse – such as chicory, radicchio, celery and bok-choy – are favourites. Make a choice from what looks tempting in the market on that particular day. At a pinch, a packet of pre-washed gourmet greens can save the day, much as I deplore their price and mediocre quality.

There isn't much time to hard-boil and shell eggs, and certainly we can't embark on skinning tomatoes or chopping more than one or two onions. So be prepared for the hearty old-fashioned textures of vegetables with peel and seeds, for the crunch of blanched cabbage and lightly cooked peppers. Flavours will be vivid and fresh, as there's little time for ingredients to marinate and mellow. One step must never be omitted, however – that of tasting the salad after tossing with dressing. Getting the right balance of flavours is essential.

250 ml /8 fl oz dry white wine

2-3 sprigs of thyme

1 bay leaf

625 g /1¼ lb scallops

1 large head of butterhead
lettuce or 2 heads
of Little Gem

3 spring onions

4 plum tomatoes

for the dressing:

2 tablespoons sherry vinegar
or red wine vinegar

1 tablespoon ground cumin

1 teaspoon crushed dried
hot red chilli pepper

5 tablespoons walnut
or olive oil

salt and freshly ground
black pepper

Scallop salad with cumin dressing

This mix of scallops, spring onions and tomato – spiced with cumin and chilli – is an inspired combination. For a more sustaining salad, add some boiled new potatoes.

1 Put 375 ml /12 fl oz water in a medium saucepan with the wine, thyme and bay leaf. Bring to a simmer.

2 Meanwhile, drain the scallops, adding any juice to the poaching liquid. Remove the tough crescent-shaped muscle from the side of each one. Add the scallops to the poaching liquid and bring just back to a simmer, stirring. Take off the heat and leave the scallops to stand in the liquid.

3 Trim the lettuce and separate the leaves; wash and dry, then refrigerate.

4 To make the dressing, in a bowl, whisk the vinegar with the cumin, chilli, salt and pepper. Gradually whisk in the oil so the dressing emulsifies. Check the seasoning.

5 Trim the spring onions, slice them at an angle and add to the dressing. Core, halve and deseed the tomatoes, then dice and add to the dressing.

6 Drain the scallops and add to the dressing, discarding the thyme and bay leaf. Toss to mix, then cover and chill the salad for at least 1 hour before serving.

7 Arrange the lettuce leaves on individual plates. Check the seasoning of the salad, then pile on to the lettuce to serve.

time in kitchen **10 minutes**   serves **4**

total cooking time 1–2 minutes | standing time at least 1 hour

This warm pasta salad is inspired by the classic Salade Niçoise. Pasta takes the place of potatoes and the tuna is freshly grilled. If you are in a real rush, use canned tuna.

1 Preheat the grill. Bring a large covered pan of salted water to the boil.

2 To make the dressing, peel the garlic, chop it and put it in a small bowl with the lemon juice, thyme, mustard and seasoning. Gradually whisk in the oil so it emulsifies. Adjust the seasoning.

3 Cook the pasta in the boiling salted water for 5-7 minutes, until al dente – tender but firm to the bite.

4 Meanwhile, brush both sides of the tuna steaks with dressing and set on the grill rack. Grill 5 cm /2 in from the heat for about 2 minutes until browned. Turn and cook for 1-2 minutes for rare tuna, or 2-3 minutes for better done.

5 Wash and dry the salad leaves and arrange in a large bowl. Chop the anchovies and stir into the remaining dressing.

6 When the tuna is cooked, remove from grill and set aside. Drain the cooked pasta and return to the pan. Add the dressing with the olives and toss to mix. Adjust the seasoning, adding more thyme, mustard, salt or pepper.

7 Pile the pasta salad into the bowl, set the tuna steaks on top and surround with the tomatoes. Serve warm.

Warm **provençal** salad of **fresh tuna**

4 boneless tuna steaks (about 625 g /1¼ lb in total)

500 g /1 lb macaroni

few lettuce or spinach leaves, or sprigs of watercress

8 anchovy fillets

125 g /4 oz black olives (preferably small Niçoise olives)

500 g /1 lb cherry tomatoes

for the dressing:

2 garlic cloves

juice of 2 lemons

1 teaspoon dried thyme

2 teaspoons Dijon-style mustard

175 ml /6 fl oz olive oil

salt and pepper

time in kitchen **12 minutes**   serves **4**

total cooking time 5–7 minutes

Wilted frisée & bacon salad

175 g /6 oz thickly sliced lean smoked bacon

1 tablespoon oil

1 medium head of frisée or escarole (about 750 g /1½ lb)

3 tablespoons red wine vinegar

3 tablespoons Cognac

freshly ground black pepper

This hot bacon and vinegar dressing effectively wilts the frisée or escarole to delicious effect. A dash of Cognac is added to cut the bacon fat and raise the spirits. To make the salad a main course, add a hard-boiled egg or two.

1 Cut the bacon into strips, or 'lardons'. Put the lardons and oil in a frying pan over a medium heat and fry until the fat is rendered and the bacon is starting to brown.

2 Meanwhile, trim the frisée or escarole, discarding the tough outer dark green leaves. Separate the remaining leaves. Wash if necessary and dry. Transfer to a salad bowl.

3 Continue to cook the bacon until crisp if you like. Discard excess fat, retaining about 3 tablespoons in the pan. Pour the hot fat and bacon over the salad leaves and toss well.

4 Add the vinegar to the frying pan and cook, stirring to dissolve the sediment, until reduced by about half.

5 Off the heat, add the Cognac and set alight, standing well back. When the flames die down, pour the dressing over the salad leaves and toss again. Add pepper to taste and serve at once.

time in kitchen **8 minutes**   serves **4**

total cooking time 5–6 minutes

Sweet peppers with pepperoni & rocket

2 large red peppers

2 large green peppers

2 large yellow peppers

125 ml /4 fl oz olive oil

2 bunches of rocket

2 garlic cloves, chopped

250 g /½ lb sliced pepperoni sausage

20 g /⅔ oz capers

3 tablespoons red wine vinegar, or more if needed

salt and freshly ground black pepper

Sweet peppers, spicy sausage and peppery rocket are an excellent combination. Be sure to buy the best pepperoni from the deli and have it sliced for you. With the addition of scrambled eggs, this salad makes a delicious brunch.

1 Halve, core and deseed the peppers, then cut each half into 5 or 6 strips. Heat the oil in the wok until very hot. Add the peppers with salt and pepper. Cook, tossing from time to time, for 6-8 minutes until softened and tinged with brown. Meanwhile, trim the rocket, wash and dry.

2 Add the garlic to the peppers and continue frying for 2-3 minutes. Stir in the pepperoni and leave over a low heat for 1 minute to allow the flavours to blend.

3 Drain the capers, rinse them under cold running water and add to the peppers with the vinegar. Take off the heat, stir and adjust the seasoning. If time, leave to marinate at this stage for about 30 minutes. Check the seasoning.

4 To serve, arrange the rocket leaves in a shallow bowl or on individual plates. Pile the salad on top to serve.

time in kitchen **14 minutes**   serves **4**

total cooking time 9–12 minutes | standing time 30 minutes

time in kitchen **14 minutes**

total cooking time 1–2 minutes

serves **4**

This salad can be varied to taste: try raspberries in place of mango, or use more delicate mixed salad leaves instead of the cos. The only rule is to maintain the basic proportions, and to use nut oil and a fruit vinegar in the dressing.

1 Trim and separate the lettuce leaves, then wash and dry. Arrange the small inner leaves around 4 individual plates. Coarsely shred the larger leaves and put into a bowl.

2 Peel the mango and slice the flesh away from the stone. Dice and set aside.

3 For the dressing, whisk half of the vinegar in a small bowl with seasoning. Gradually whisk in all but 2 tablespoons of the oil, so the dressing emulsifies. Adjust the seasoning.

Crazy **salad**

**1 large head of cos lettuce
(about 500 g /1 lb)**

1 mango

**125 g /4 oz peeled cooked
baby prawns**

125 g /4 oz chicken livers

60 g /2 oz walnut pieces

for the dressing:

**4 tablespoons raspberry or
sherry vinegar**

125 ml / 4 fl oz walnut oil

**salt and freshly ground
black pepper**

4 Add the prawns to the dressing, toss to mix, then add to the shredded lettuce and stir until well coated. Check the seasoning. Pile the shredded lettuce and prawns on each plate. Scatter the diced mango on top.

5 Heat the remaining oil in a small frying pan. Cut the chicken livers into 3 or 4 slices, discarding any membrane, and sprinkle with salt and pepper. Add to the hot oil and fry, stirring, over a high heat for 1-2 minutes, until brown on the outside but still pink in the centre.

6 Add the remaining vinegar and cook for 15 seconds, stirring to deglaze the pan. Spoon the livers over the salad, sprinkle with the walnuts and serve, while still warm.

15 g /½ oz butter

1 spring onion

60 g /2 oz mushrooms

1 slice of white bread

15 g /½ oz blue cheese

30 g /1 oz dried figs

4 skinless, boneless chicken breasts

salt and freshly ground black pepper

for the salad:

small bunch of rocket

small head of radicchio

for the dressing:

1 teaspoon Dijon-style mustard

2 tablespoons red wine vinegar

125 ml /4 fl oz olive oil

Fig-stuffed chicken salad with blue cheese

For this unusual Californian salad the chicken can be served warm or cold, on its bed of peppery salad leaves.

1 Preheat the oven to 190°C/375°F/gas 5. Butter a medium baking dish.

2 Heat the remaining butter in a frying pan. While it heats, trim the spring onion and slice it across at an angle. Add to the pan and sauté gently for 1-2 minutes to soften.

3 Meanwhile, trim off the mushroom stalks and wipe the caps. Put in a food processor and pulse to chop finely. Add to the spring onion with salt and pepper and cook over a fairly high heat for 2-3 minutes until tender and their liquid has evaporated.

4 Tear the bread into 2 or 3 pieces, put in the processor and work to fine crumbs. Off the heat, add to the mushrooms and crumble in the cheese. Trim the figs, chop them and add. Season with pepper to taste, and a little salt if needed.

5 With a small sharp knife, cut a deep horizontal pocket in each chicken breast, being careful not to cut right through. Spoon the stuffing into the pockets. Transfer to the baking dish, season and cover tightly with foil. Bake for 30-35 minutes, or until the chicken breasts are cooked through.

6 Meanwhile, rinse and dry the rocket. Trim the radicchio and shred coarsely. Put the leaves in a bowl.

7 To make the dressing, combine the mustard, vinegar and seasoning in a small bowl. Gradually whisk in the oil so the dressing emulsifies. Check the seasoning.

8 Serve the chicken hot or cold: sliced and arrange on 4 plates; drizzle with half of the dressing. Toss the salad in the remaining dressing and pile next to the chicken.

time in kitchen **11 minutes**   serves **4**

total cooking time 35–40 minutes

1 medium cucumber

750 g /1½ lb very ripe
beefsteak tomatoes

500 g /1 lb loaf of ciabatta or
crusty country bread

2 mild red onions

250-375 g /½ - ¾ lb prosciutto

for the dressing:

1 garlic clove

3 tablespoons balsamic
vinegar, or to taste

4 tablespoons olive oil,
or to taste

large bunch of fresh basil

salt and freshly ground
black pepper

Panzanella

For this Tuscan salad you need the ripest of tomatoes, aromatic fresh basil, the fruitiest of olive oil, sweet balsamic vinegar and rustic Italian bread. Day-old bread is fine.

1 To make the dressing, peel the garlic, chop it finely and put in a small bowl with the vinegar, salt and pepper. Gradually whisk in the oil to emulsify. Pull the leaves from the basil, shred the leaves, then add to the dressing.

2 Peel, halve and deseed the cucumber, then dice the flesh. Remove the cores from the tomatoes, then chop. Cut the bread into 2.5 cm /1 in cubes, retaining the crust; set aside. Peel the onions and cut into small dice.

3 Put the cucumber, tomato and onion in a large bowl. Add the dressing and mix gently. Add the bread cubes and toss to mix. Leave for 5 minutes to let the flavours develop.

4 Meanwhile, arrange the prosciutto on 4 individual plates. Season the salad generously with pepper. Taste and adjust the seasoning, adding more oil, vinegar or salt if you like. Pile it on the plates and serve at room temperature within an hour for optimum flavour.

time in kitchen **10 minutes**   serves **4**

standing time 5 minutes

This adaptation of a rustic Greek salad features juicy baby tomatoes, goats' cheese instead of Feta, handfuls of home-grown herbs and fat black olives from Nyons in Provence. To make the salad go further, serve it on a bed of couscous, which takes almost no time to prepare.

1 Halve the cucumbers lengthwise, deseed and dice the flesh. Place in a large bowl with the tomatoes. Halve, core and deseed the peppers, then roughly dice and add to the bowl. Thinly slice the onion into rings and add to the salad. Dice the cheese and add that with the olives.

2 To make the dressing, combine the vinegar, pepper and a little salt in a bowl. Gradually whisk in the oil so the dressing emulsifies. Check the seasoning.

3 Pour the dressing over the salad and toss gently. Taste and adjust the seasoning again. Take the herb leaves from the stems and coarsely chop. Scatter over the salad and toss lightly. Serve at once or, if time, leave to stand in a cool place for 1-2 hours to allow the flavours to mellow before serving.

Burgundian **Greek salad**

2 medium cucumbers

250 g /½ lb cherry tomatoes

2 green peppers

2 medium sweet onions

500 g /1 lb firm goats' cheese or Feta

150 g /5 oz black oil-cured olives

small bunch of basil

small bunch of flat-leaf parsley

for the dressing:

3 tablespoons red wine vinegar

125 ml /4 fl oz olive oil

salt and freshly ground black pepper

time in kitchen **12 minutes**   serves **4**

standing time 1–2 hours, if possible

½ head of red cabbage
(about 500 g /1 lb)

125 ml /4 fl oz red wine
vinegar

1 large tart green apple

75 g /2½ oz Roquefort cheese

for the dressing:

1 tablespoon Dijon-style
mustard

3 tablespoons red wine
vinegar

175 ml /6 fl oz walnut oil

salt and freshly ground
black pepper

Red cabbage, apple & roquefort salad

Even in winter, red cabbage can be relied on to be crisp and colourful. It discolours easily, however, so care must be taken to preserve its vivid leaves. Use a stainless-steel knife or mandoline for shredding, and toss with an acid ingredient – in this case wine vinegar – to set the colour.

1 Bring a covered medium pan of water to the boil. Meanwhile, trim, core and finely shred the cabbage, discarding any thick ribs. Put the cabbage in a large bowl.

2 Bring the vinegar to the boil, then pour over the cabbage and mix well – the cabbage will turn bright red.

3 Remove the pan of boiling water from the heat, add the cabbage, cover and leave for 2-3 minutes to soften.

4 Meanwhile, to make the dressing, combine the mustard, vinegar, salt and pepper in a small bowl. Gradually whisk in the walnut oil, so the dressing emulsifies.

5 Quarter and core the apple, and peel if you prefer. Cut into chunks, then immediately toss in the dressing to prevent discoloration.

6 Drain the cabbage in a colander, pat dry with kitchen paper and replace in the bowl. Add the apple with the dressing, toss well and adjust the seasoning. Cover and leave to stand in the refrigerator for at least 15 minutes, up to 4 hours if possible, to allow the flavours to mellow.

7 Crumble the Roquefort over the salad to serve.

time in kitchen **10 minutes**   serves **4**

standing time 15 minutes, or up to 4 hours if possible

This recipe has become a classic – a staple in bistros from Lyon to Los Angeles – with varying salad leaves. For a starter serve one round of toast per person as here, or increase to three for a summer lunch.

1 Preheat the grill. In the meantime, make the dressing. Combine the mustard, vinegar, salt and pepper in a small bowl. Gradually whisk in the olive oil, so the dressing emulsifies. Check the seasoning.

2 Cut the goats' cheese into 4 rounds. Cut four 1 cm /½ in thick rounds from the bread. Brush with dressing and place on a baking sheet. Slice the olives, spread them on the bread and set a slice of cheese on top, to cover the bread completely; if necessary spread to the edges with a knife or the bread will scorch.

3 Brush with dressing and grill 7.5 cm /3 in from the heat for 3-5 minutes until the cheese is melted and browned.

4 Meanwhile, trim the chicory and cut into 2 cm /¾ in diagonal slices; place in a large bowl. Remove the stems from the watercress, then add to the chicory. Drizzle with the dressing, toss to mix and check the seasoning.

5 Pile the salad on to 4 serving plates. Set a round of goats' cheese toast on each salad and serve at once.

Chicory salad with goats' cheese toasts

2 small goats' cheeses or 1 small log (about 175 g /6 oz)

½ loaf of French bread

2 tablespoons stoned black or green olives

2 heads (about 375 g /¾ lb) of chicory

large bunch of watercress

for the dressing:

1 teaspoon Dijon-style mustard

2 tablespoons raspberry or red wine vinegar

6 tablespoons olive oil

salt and freshly ground black pepper

time in kitchen **8 minutes**   serves **4**

total cooking time 3–5 minutes

Caponata

125 ml /4 fl oz red wine vinegar

1 tablespoon sugar

75 g /2½ oz pitted green olives

30 g /1 oz capers

2 onions

3½ tablespoons olive oil

1 small head of celery

2 medium aubergines (about 1 kg /2 lb in total)

250 g /8 oz can chopped tomatoes

1 tablespoon tomato paste

salt and freshly ground black pepper

This sweet-and-sour combination originates from Sicily. Look for small, thin aubergines, which have an intense flavour. Caponata is the perfect accompaniment to charcoal-grilled sardines or tuna.

1 Put the vinegar, sugar, olives and drained capers in a small saucepan over a low heat and simmer for 3-5 minutes.

2 Meanwhile, halve and thinly slice the onions. Heat 2 tablespoons of the oil in a wok, add the onions with salt and pepper and cook over medium heat to soften. Trim and thinly slice the celery, then add to the onions.

3 Trim and chop the aubergines into 1 cm /½ in pieces. Add the remaining olive oil to the wok. Stir in the aubergines with more salt and pepper, increase the heat and cook, stirring, for 2-3 minutes until starting to soften.

4 Stir in the chopped tomatoes, tomato paste, vinegar, capers and olives. Reduce the heat to medium, cover and cook for 10-12 minutes until all the vegetables are very tender. Transfer to a bowl and leave to cool for 30 minutes.

5 Check the seasoning and serve the caponata at room temperature, or chilled if you prefer, either in a large salad bowl or on individual plates.

time in kitchen **10 minutes** serves **4**

total cooking time 10–12 minutes | standing time 30 minutes

Chapter 5

not quite

vegetarian

Some of the recipes in this chapter are indeed vegetarian and one or two, such as Provençal Tricolor and Roast Root Vegetables with Walnuts, are even vegan, but most rely on ham or bacon – or perhaps chicken stock – to bolster flavour. Several feature cheese in off-beat recipes like Plum Tomato and Oregano Frittata, and Blue Cheese Puff – a giant batter pudding. With their emphasis on vegetables, they are light as well as healthy and nutritious – and a complete meal in themselves.

We're all eating this way nowadays, whether for health reasons or, as in my case, for the pleasure of exploring the many different tastes and textures of vegetables and fruits.

We can all profit from the revolution in year-round supplies, with exotica like okra, celeriac and even beansprouts now commonplace in many markets. The recipe for Roast Root Vegetables with Walnuts offers a chance to try out a new root such as salsify or Japanese artichoke. For that matter, any type of squash can take the place of pumpkin in Baked Pumpkin with Plums & Bacon.

So in this chapter I hope you'll embark on some experiments. Baked eggs can be flavoured with all sorts of vegetables besides spring onions, and a frittata begs for a filling of whatever vegetables you have to hand. Just be sure what you buy is fresh, preferably in season.

Baked pumpkin with plums & bacon

250 g /½ lb thickly sliced bacon

100 g /3½ oz butter

500 g /1 lb purple plums

1.4 kg /3 lb pieces of pumpkin

1 tablespoon brown sugar

1 teaspoon ground cinnamon

1 teaspoon ground allspice

½ teaspoon salt

½ teaspoon freshly ground black pepper

The sweet and savoury combination of pumpkin and plums marries with salty bacon, sugar and spice. A grain pilaf makes a good accompaniment. Other winter squash, such as butternut, can be used.

1 Preheat the oven to 190°C/375°F/gas 5. Dice the bacon. Heat 15 g /½ oz of the butter in a frying pan, add the bacon and sauté for 5-7 minutes over medium heat until browned and slightly crisp.

2 Meanwhile, halve and stone the plums. Put them in a large bowl.

3 Remove the seeds, fibres and skin from the pumpkin, then cut into 2.5 cm /1 in cubes; you should have 825 g /1¾ lb prepared weight. Add the pumpkin to the plums.

4 Add the remaining butter to the sautéed bacon and melt over a low heat. Stir in the sugar, cinnamon, allspice, salt and pepper. Add to the plums and pumpkin and stir to mix.

5 Spread the mixture in a shallow baking dish and cover with foil (or put in a microwave dish and cover with film). Bake in the oven for 50-60 minutes (or microwave on high for 10-12 minutes). Serve piping hot.

time in kitchen **14 minutes**   serves **4**

total cooking time 50–60 minutes (10–12 in microwave)

150 g /5 oz piece of lean
bacon

2 tablespoons vegetable oil

2 onions

4 carrots

500 g /1 lb lentils

3 bay leaves

1 tablespoon salt, or to taste

1 teaspoon freshly ground
black pepper, or to taste

20 g /¾ oz coriander seeds

Lentils with coriander & bacon

Large brown lentils are best for this casserole, which makes a simple main dish or a good accompaniment to game or pork. There's no need to soak the lentils before cooking.

1 Dice the bacon. Heat the oil in a heavy casserole and sauté the bacon over medium heat. Meanwhile, halve and thinly slice the onions. Add to the bacon and continue sautéing. Dice the carrots, then stir in.

2 Wash the lentils in a colander under cold water, then stir into the bacon and vegetables. Add 1 litre /1⅔ pt water, the bay leaves, salt and pepper. Cover and bring to the boil. Meanwhile, coarsely crush the coriander seeds and stir into the lentils.

3 Lower the heat, partially cover and simmer gently for 1-1½ hours, depending on the type of lentils, until tender and the water is absorbed. If necessary, add a little extra water towards the end of cooking.

4 Discard the bay leaves and adjust the seasoning to serve.

time in kitchen **13 minutes**   serves **4**

total cooking time about 1–1½ hours

Eggs '*en cocotte*' – baked in a ramekin topped with cream – are a rarity these days, but delicious and quick. They may be flavoured with prawns, sautéed mushrooms, or spring onions and croûtons as here. Serve with strips of toast.

1 Preheat the oven to 190°C/375°F/gas 5. Lay a folded tea-towel in a large roasting pan and pour in a 2.5 cm/1 in depth of water. Bring to the boil on the hob.

2 Meanwhile, melt 30 g /1 oz of the butter in a frying pan over a low heat. Trim the spring onions and thinly slice at an angle. Stir into the butter, season and cook gently for 4-5 minutes until soft and lightly browned.

3 Meanwhile, for the croûtons, melt the remaining butter in a large frying pan over a low heat. Trim the crusts off the bread and cut the bread into cubes. Add to the butter and fry, stirring constantly, until evenly browned. Drain on kitchen paper.

4 Spoon the spring onions into 8 ramekins and top with the croûtons. Season generously with salt and pepper. Break an egg into each ramekin and top with a tablespoon of cream.

5 Stand the ramekins on the cloth in the water bath. Bring the water back to the boil, then transfer to the oven. Bake for 12-15 minutes, until the egg whites are almost set. They will continue cooking for 1-2 minutes in the residual heat.

6 Transfer the ramekins to 4 individual plates to serve. The egg whites should be just set and the yolks still soft.

Baked **eggs** with **onions & croutons**

125 g /4 oz butter

4 spring onions

4 slices of white bread

8 eggs

125 ml /4 fl oz double cream

salt and freshly ground black pepper

time in kitchen **12 minutes**   serves **4**

total cooking time 17–20 minutes

Plum tomato & oregano frittata

2 tablespoons olive oil

1 onion

2 garlic cloves

500 g /1 lb plum tomatoes

7 eggs

45 g /1½ oz grated Gruyère cheese

large bunch of fresh oregano

30 g /1 oz butter

salt and freshly ground black pepper

Unlike a traditional omelette, the Italian *frittata* is cooked slowly, so the eggs gently puff and set to a golden cake that is served hot or cold, cut into wedges. A frittata can be flavoured with assorted vegetables and cheese, meat or fish. Italian-style country bread is the perfect complement.

1 Heat the olive oil in a 25-30 cm/ 10-12 in heavy-based frying pan or omelette pan over a low heat. Halve and thinly slice the onion, add to the oil and sauté over a medium heat to soften. Peel the garlic, chop and stir into the onion.

2 Core, deseed and dice the tomatoes. Stir into the onion mixture, season and cook for 1-2 minutes, to soften slightly.

3 Meanwhile whisk the eggs in a large bowl, with salt and pepper, until smooth and slightly frothy. Stir in the hot tomato mixture, together with the cheese and oregano leaves stripped from the stems.

4 Wipe out the frying pan, return to the heat and add the butter. Heat until foaming, then pour in the egg mixture. Cover with a lid and cook over a very low heat for 25-35 minutes until puffed, set on top and browned underneath.

5 Run a knife around the edge of the frittata to loosen it and invert on to a large warmed plate. Serve hot or at room temperature, cut into wedges.

time in kitchen **13 minutes**   serves **4**

total cooking time 30–40 minutes

This simple, giant puff is really a cross between a cheese choux pastry and a soufflé. You can bake it in one large dish as here, or in ramekins, which cook in just 15-20 minutes. Serve with a salad of bitter greens.

1 Preheat the oven to 190°C/375°F/gas 5. Generously butter a 2 litre /3¼ pt shallow soufflé dish or deep baking dish.

2 Put the milk and 30 g /1 oz of the butter in a medium saucepan and bring to the boil.

3 Mix the flour with all but 1 tablespoon of the Parmesan or Gruyère, and a little pepper in a bowl. When the milk boils, take the pan off the heat and immediately tip in the flour mix, stirring vigorously with a whisk until the mixture is smooth and thick. Crumble in the blue cheese; whisk well.

4 Return the pan to the heat and cook, whisking constantly, just until the blue cheese melts. Take off the heat and whisk in the eggs, one at a time. Adjust the seasoning.

5 Pour the mixture into the prepared dish. Dot with the remaining butter and sprinkle with the reserved cheese. Bake for 30-40 minutes until puffed and brown; the edges should be crisp and the centre slightly soft. Serve at once.

Blue cheese puff

45 g /1½ oz butter, plus extra for greasing dish

250 ml /8 fl oz milk

30 g /1 oz flour

100 g /3¼ oz grated Parmesan or Gruyère cheese

125 g /4 oz blue Stilton or Gorgonzola cheese

3 eggs

freshly ground black pepper

time in kitchen **11 minutes**   serves **4**
total cooking time 30–40 minutes

Grated **potato & cheese** gratin

30 g /1 oz butter

150 ml /5 fl oz double cream

125 g /4 oz cream cheese

3 eggs

5-6 sprigs of rosemary, sage or thyme

125 g /4 oz grated Gruyère cheese

2 tablespoons marc or Cognac (optional)

½ teaspoon freshly grated nutmeg

750 g /1½ lb floury baking potatoes

salt and pepper

This batter bakes to a deliciously crisp cake with a soft centre, and begs for additions such as slivers of ham or cooked chicken, chunks of walnut or toasted hazelnuts. It is an ideal winter dish, good with a salad of escarole.

1 Preheat the oven to 200°C/400°F/gas 6. Spread the butter in a 2 litre /3¼ pt shallow baking dish or microwave dish.

2 In a large bowl, whisk the cream into the cream cheese until soft. Add the eggs and whisk again until smooth.

3 Strip the herb leaves from the stems. Chop the rosemary finely; if using sage or thyme, chop coarsely. Stir the chopped herbs into the batter, together with the grated cheese, marc or Cognac if using, and nutmeg. Season liberally with salt and pepper.

4 Grate the potatoes, using a food processor fitted with a coarse grating disc. Stir into the batter and adjust the seasoning.

5 Spread the potato mixture in the prepared dish to form a layer about 2.5 cm /1 in deep. Bake in the oven for about 40-50 minutes until crisp and golden brown on top. (Alternatively, microwave on high for 14-18 minutes, then brown under the grill.) Serve hot, cut into wedges.

time in kitchen **7 minutes**   serves **4-6**

total cooking time 40–50 minutes (14–18 in microwave)

butter for greasing dish

2 garlic cloves

125 g /4 oz lean sliced bacon

125 g /4 oz cooked country ham

1 onion

large bunch of parsley

175 g /6 oz washed spinach

90 g /3 oz flour

500 ml /16 fl oz milk

4 eggs

¼ teaspoon grated nutmeg

freshly ground black pepper

Pounti

A type of flan, *pounti* comes from the Auvergne, where it is often eaten cold as a snack. I prefer to serve it warm from the oven, as a meal in itself. Other vegetables can take the place of spinach, such as rocket, Swiss chard or curly kale.

1 Preheat the oven to 175°C /350°F/gas 4. Butter a 1.75 litre /2 ⅔ pt shallow baking dish or microwave dish.

2 Peel the onion and garlic. Cut the bacon, ham and onion into chunks and put them in the food processor with the garlic. Pulse until coarsely chopped. Strip the parsley leaves from the stems and process until quite finely chopped. Tip the mixture into a large bowl.

3 Remove the stalks from the spinach and coarsely chop in the processor, in two batches. Stir into the bacon mixture.

4 Put the flour in a bowl, make a well in the middle and add the milk. Stir with a whisk, gradually drawing in the flour, until smooth. Whisk in the eggs until the batter is smooth. Add the nutmeg and season liberally with pepper – the bacon and ham will add sufficient salt.

5 Stir the batter into the bacon and spinach mixture, then pour into the prepared dish. Bake on a baking sheet in the oven for 50-60 minutes, until browned and set in the centre. (Alternatively microwave, with the dish tightly covered with film, on medium high for 20-23 minutes.)

6 Leave to stand for 5 minutes before serving, cut into wedges. Pounti is also good eaten cold.

time in kitchen **11 minutes** serves **4**

total cooking time 50–60 minutes (20–23 in microwave)

The colours of this dish instantly evoke Provence. Other vegetables can be added – such as quartered sweet peppers, thinly sliced sweet onions, sliced pumpkin or butternut squash – to turn the dish into a meal in itself. It is also an ideal accompaniment for roast or grilled lamb.

1 Preheat the oven to 190°C/375°F/gas 5. Peel the garlic and strip the herb leaves from the stems. Put the garlic, herbs and half of the olive oil in a food processor and pulse for about 15-20 seconds to chop the herbs coarsely. Spread the mixture in a rectangular baking dish, measuring about 23 x 33 cm /9 x 13 in.

2 Cut the aubergine and tomatoes into 1 cm /½ in slices, discarding the ends. Cut the courgettes into slightly thinner slices. Sprinkle with salt and pepper and arrange the vegetables overlapping and almost upright in the dish.

3 Drizzle with remaining oil and bake for 30-40 minutes, until the vegetables are tender and lightly browned. If they seem dry during baking, sprinkle with a little more oil.

4 Serve hot, or at room temperature sprinkled with a little lemon juice.

Provençal tricolor

3 garlic cloves

generous bunch of mixed herbs, such as rosemary, thyme, basil, sage and oregano

125 ml /4 fl oz olive oil, or as required

1 medium aubergine (about 750 g /1½ lb)

2 large tomatoes (about 750 g /1½ lb)

2 medium courgettes (about 500 g /1 lb)

juice of ½ lemon, or to taste

salt and freshly ground black pepper

time in kitchen **12 minutes**   serves **4**

total cooking time 30–40 minutes

1 onion

4 tablespoons olive oil

1 medium aubergine (about 375 g /¾ lb)

2 garlic cloves

1 tablespoon ground coriander

1 teaspoon dried Provençal herbs or dried thyme

1 red pepper

1 green pepper

500 g /1 lb plum tomatoes

2 small courgettes (about 375 g /¾ lb)

small bunch of basil

salt and freshly ground black pepper

Quick ratatouille

Make ratatouille in summer when aubergines, peppers, courgettes and tomatoes are at their best. Serve it hot, chilled or at room temperature – on its own as a light main course, or as an accompaniment to grilled fish or chicken.

1 Peel, halve and thinly slice the onion. Heat 2 tablespoons oil in the wok and fry the onion over a medium heat to soften.

2 Trim the aubergine and cut into generous chunks, about 1 cm / ½ in. Stir into the onion with the remaining oil, season generously and continue cooking.

3 Chop the garlic and add to the wok with the coriander and dried herbs. Halve, core and deseed the peppers, then slice thinly. Stir into the other vegetables.

4 Halve, deseed and chop the tomatoes, then add to the wok. Cut the courgettes into 1 cm /⅜ in slices. Stir them into the other vegetables and adjust the seasoning.

5 Cover the wok and cook over a medium heat for a further 8-10 minutes until all the vegetables are softened, but still holding their shape. Meanwhile, strip the basil leaves from the stems and coarsely shred.

6 Stir the basil into the ratatouille. Serve hot, or leave to stand for at least 30 minutes to cool to room temperature. Ratatouille can be refrigerated for up to 2 days. Taste and adjust the seasoning just before serving.

time in kitchen **12 minutes**   serves **4**

total cooking time 15–18 minutes

4 medium carrots (about 250 g /½ lb)

2 turnips or ½ head of celeriac (about 250 g /½ lb)

about 250 g /½ lb baby beetroot

3 medium potatoes (about 500 g /1 lb)

125 ml /4 fl oz walnut oil or vegetable oil

8 shallots (unpeeled)

8 garlic cloves (unpeeled)

2 teaspoons sugar

1 teaspoon nutmeg

½ teaspoon allspice

60 g /2 oz walnut pieces

1 teaspoon salt

½ teaspoon pepper

Roast **root vegetables** with **walnuts**

Lightly spiced, sweet roast vegetables make a wonderful accompaniment to any grilled or roast meat. Vegetables that cook quickly, such as potatoes, should be cut into larger pieces than those, like carrots, which take longer.

1 Preheat the oven to 200°C/400°F/gas 6. Trim the carrots, turnips or celeriac and the beetroot, leaving a little of the green tops. Scrub these vegetables and the potatoes clean in cold water; dry well.

2 Put the oil into a large flameproof roasting pan and set over a medium heat. As you cut each vegetable, add it to the pan. Quarter carrots and turnips lengthwise. If using celeriac, cut into 4 wedges and halve each wedge. Add the beetroot whole, and the shallots and garlic in their skins.

3 Mix the sugar, nutmeg, allspice, walnuts, salt and pepper together in a small bowl. Sprinkle over the vegetables and toss until well coated.

4 Cover the roasting pan with foil and roast for 45-55 minutes, stirring occasionally, until the vegetables are tender and browned. Serve hot.

time in kitchen **10 minutes**   serves **4**

total cooking time 45–55 minutes

fast

1 2 3 4 5 6 7 8 9 10 11 12 13 14 15 1 2 3 4 5 6 7 8 9 10 11 12 13 14 15 1 2 3 4 5 6 7 8 9 10 11 12 13 14 15

finishes

One reason why desserts give so much pleasure is that they are a luxury rather than a necessity. Some of the easy ideas in this chapter are scarcely more complicated than the traditional French ending to a meal – cheese and fruit. For instance, in no time you can macerate seasonal fruits in caramel or honey, or poach pears in a spiced red wine syrup.

Moving a step further, whipping egg whites or cream in a mixer brings within reach a simple Chocolate Mousse, or a Raspberry Fool layered with berries and chocolate. We can even prepare a quick Breton Butter Cake, which calls for only four ingredients – all storecupboard staples. For a special occasion, a soufflé can be whipped up astonishingly fast.

Conventional tarts and pies aren't feasible within our 15-minute limit, as the pastry takes too long, but frozen filo pastry dough is another matter. With a discreet brushing of butter, it will bake to a flaky crispness. Use it here to make a strudel filled with cherries, cinnamon and brown sugar, or a Moroccan galette stuffed with dried fruit and chocolate.

If expecting guests, prepare your dessert ahead. All the cold desserts can be made the night before. The hot desserts are quick to prepare, but – with the exception of Strawberry Burnt Cream – they do take time to cook. So it's lucky they come at the end of the meal. After a leisurely main course, even Plum Batter Pudding will be cooked to perfection!

100 g /3¼ oz sugar

l bottle (750 ml /1¼ pt) fruity red wine

1 cinnamon stick

1 tablespoon black peppercorns

pared zest of 1 lemon

4 large, firm pears with stalks (about 1 kg /2 lb)

Peppered **pears** in **red wine**

This recipe will fill your kitchen with the warm spicy smell of mulled wine. Serve the pears warm in winter, with a slice of Breton Butter Cake (see page 127) or crisp ginger biscuits. In summer, serve them chilled with vanilla ice-cream.

1 Put the sugar, wine, cinnamon stick, peppercorns and lemon zest in a small pan (just big enough to hold the pears). Heat gently until the sugar is dissolved, then slowly bring to the boil, stirring once or twice. (Alternatively microwave in a suitable bowl on high for 3 minutes.)

2 Meanwhile, peel the pears, retaining the stalks, and scoop out the bases. Immediately immerse in the syrup, standing them upright if possible. Set a heavy heatproof plate on top of the pears to keep them immersed.

3 Bring the syrup almost to a simmer and poach the pears very gently for 30-40 minutes, until translucent and tender. Cooking time varies, depending on the variety and ripeness. (Or microwave, covered, on high for 10-12 minutes.)

4 Transfer the pears to a bowl, cutting a sliver from their bases if necessary so they sit upright. Return the syrup to the heat and boil uncovered for 7-10 minutes until dark and enriched, but not sticky. Strain over the pears to serve.

Spiced **figs** in **red wine**

Replace the pears with 12 purple or green figs. Substitute a 2.5 cm/ 1 in piece of fresh ginger, sliced, for the peppercorns. Poach the figs for 4-6 minutes only. Trim the stems and cut a deep cross in each fig before straining on the reduced syrup. Serve warm or chilled, with cream cheese or yogurt.

time in kitchen **8 minutes**   serves **4**

total cooking time 40–55 minutes (20–25 using microwave)

As ready-made filo dough is infinitely quicker to use than authentic strudel pastry this can be assembled in minutes. Serve it warm or at room temperature, with soured cream.

1 Preheat the oven to 190°C/375°F/gas 5. Melt the butter and finely grate the lemon zest. Mix the lemon zest with the brown sugar and cinnamon in a small bowl. Drain the cherries.

2 Lay a dry tea-towel on the work surface, short side nearest you. Unwrap the filo and keep covered with a damp tea-towel to prevent it drying out.

3 Lay one filo sheet on the tea-towel, short end towards you, and brush with melted butter. Sprinkle with a quarter of the cherries, then a quarter of the sugar mixture. Layer the remaining filo and filling on top in the same way, brushing each filo sheet with butter.

4 Fold in the two corners of dough nearest you about 2.5 cm /1 in. Pull upwards on the front edge of the tea-towel so the dough starts to roll up fairly tightly. Continue rolling to form quite a tight cylinder. Place, seam side down, on a buttered baking sheet and brush with butter.

5 Bake for 25-30 minutes until crisp and brown, and a skewer inserted in the centre for 20 seconds is hot to the touch on removing. Leave to cool slightly on the baking sheet for about 10 minutes.

6 Serve hot or at room temperature. Just before serving, sprinkle generously with icing sugar and cut into diagonal slices with a serrated knife, discarding the ends. Serve a bowl of soured cream separately.

cherry strudel

45 g /1½ oz unsalted butter

1 lemon

60 g /2 oz brown sugar

½ teaspoon ground cinnamon

375 g /12 oz can of pitted bitter cherries

4 large sheets of filo dough (about 60 g /2 oz)

icing sugar for sprinkling

time in kitchen **11 minutes**   serves **4**

total cooking time 25–30 minutes

plum batter pudding

butter for greasing the dish

500 g /1 lb plums, or 250 g / ½ lb stoned prunes

60 g /2 oz sugar, plus more for coating dish

4 eggs

30 g /1 oz flour

pinch of salt

250 ml /8 fl oz milk

3 tablespoons slivovitz, prune or other fruit liqueur (see right)

icing sugar for sprinkling

This version of the French batter pudding 'clafoutis' uses plums or prunes rather than cherries, though you can use small bitter cherries during their short season. Apricots are another alternative. The alcohol should echo the fruit – apricot liqueur for apricots and kirsch for cherries.

1 Preheat the oven to 190°C/375°F/gas 5. Butter a 1.5 litre /2½ pt shallow baking dish, then sprinkle with sugar and tilt the dish so it is evenly coated; discard excess.

2 Halve and stone the plums, if using. Scatter the plums or prunes in a single layer in the baking dish.

3 To make the batter, whisk the eggs and sugar in a bowl for 1-2 minutes until light and frothy. Stir in the flour and salt just until smooth; do not beat. Stir in the milk. Strain the batter over the fruit.

4 Bake for 50-60 minutes until the pudding is puffed, brown and firm in the centre. Leave to stand for 5-10 minutes, then sprinkle with the alcohol. Dust generously with icing sugar and serve warm.

time in kitchen **8 minutes**   serves **4**

total cooking time 50–60 minutes | standing time 5–10 minutes

Orange salad with **caramel**

**60 g /2 oz pecan pieces or
walnut halves**

150 g /5 oz sugar

4 large navel oranges

Few desserts are more refreshing than this simple salad. Look for large navel oranges, which are seedless and perfect for slicing, or use smaller blood oranges, allowing two per person. You can make the salad up to a day ahead, but keep the caramel tightly covered otherwise it will soften.

1 Pile the nuts on to a well oiled baking sheet. Put the sugar and 125 ml /4 fl oz of water in a small heavy based pan and heat gently, without stirring, until the sugar dissolves.

2 Meanwhile, using a serrated knife, peel the oranges of all skin and white pith. Slice crosswise into 5 mm /¼ in slices, then fan out the orange slices on individual serving plates.

3 Once the sugar is dissolved, increase the heat and boil steadily, without stirring, for 5-8 minutes until the syrup starts to colour at the edge. Lower the heat slightly and cook for a further 30-60 seconds to a dark golden caramel.

4 Immediately take off the heat and pour about half the syrup over the nuts. Leave to cool and harden.

5 Quickly add 4 tablespoons of water to the remaining caramel in the pan. Heat for 1-2 minutes to dissolve the caramel and thicken the sauce slightly. Spoon over the oranges and chill for about 30 minutes.

6 When the nut caramel is set hard, place in a sturdy plastic bag and pound with a rolling pin, into small chips.

7 Just before serving, sprinkle the oranges with the nut caramel chips.

Orange salad with **honey caramel**
Omit the nuts. Substitute 150 g /5 oz honey for the sugar.

time in kitchen **14 minutes**   serves **4**
total cooking time 8–12 minutes

60 g /2 oz dark bitter chocolate

30 g /1 oz dried apricots

30 g /1 oz dried figs

75 g /2½ oz walnut pieces

60 g /2 oz unsalted butter

4 sheets of filo dough, about 30 cm /12 in square

Moroccan dried fruit & chocolate galettes

Greek filo pastry is used in place of the more robust Moroccan *brik* dough. Filo is widely available, fresh and frozen, though the sheets of dough vary in size.

1 Preheat the oven to 190°C/375°F/gas 5. Finely chop the chocolate and dried fruit. Mix together in a bowl, with the walnuts.

2 Melt the butter. Unwrap the filo and keep covered with a damp tea-towel to prevent it drying out. Lay one sheet of filo on the work surface and brush lightly with butter. Repeat with the remaining filo, to make 4 layers.

3 Cut the layered filo into four 15 cm /6 in squares. Spoon the filling evenly into the centre of each square. Draw up the corners of the filo over the filling to enclose and press together to seal. Flip the galettes over, flatten slightly and form into neat rounds.

4 Set the galettes on a buttered baking sheet and brush with butter. Cut a small hole in the top of each one to allow steam to escape. Bake for 20-25 minutes until brown and crisp. Transfer to a wire rack to cool.

5 Serve the galettes warm or cool, sprinkled with icing sugar.

time in kitchen **14 minutes**   serves **4**

total cooking time 20–25 minutes

This simple marmalade soufflé consists of a light meringue mixed with melted marmalade – lemon, orange or lime as you prefer. Shortbread is an ideal accompaniment.

1 Preheat the oven to 190°C/375°F/gas 5. Melt the butter and brush 4 large 250 ml /8 fl oz ramekins or individual soufflé dishes with it. Put the marmalade in a small pan with 4 tablespoons of water and melt over a medium heat, then remove and set aside.

2 Meanwhile, using an electric mixer on medium speed, whisk the egg whites with the salt until frothy. Increase speed to maximum and whisk for 2-3 minutes, until very stiff. With the whisk turning, pour in the sugar and continue whisking for 30-60 seconds to form a glossy meringue, which stands in peaks when the whisk is lifted.

3 Stir about a quarter of the meringue into the warm marmalade to lighten it, then carefully fold this into the remaining meringue.

4 Spoon into the prepared ramekins, forming a slight peak in the middle. Set the ramekins on a baking sheet and bake for 7-10 minutes until puffed and brown – the peak will be quite dark.

5 Set the ramekins on individual plates and serve at once.

Marmalade soufflé

15-30 g /½-1 oz butter

200 g /6½ oz fine-cut (jelly type) lemon marmalade

whites of 4 eggs

pinch of salt

60 g /2 oz caster sugar

time in kitchen **12 minutes**   serves **4**

total cooking time 7–10 minutes

Honey-baked apples with chocolate

4 medium apples (about 750 g /1½ lb)

125 g /4 oz plain chocolate

4 generous tablespoons honey (about 100 g /3¾ oz)

Baked apples are best made with a tart variety of apple that will be fluffy and juicy when baked; traditional favourites are Cox's or Reine des Reinettes, though you can always use the ubiquitous Granny Smith.

1 Preheat the oven to 190°/375°F/gas 5. Remove the cores from the apples, using an apple corer. Scoop out a larger cavity about 2.5 cm /1 in in diameter, with the corer.

2 Score the skin of each apple horizontally around its 'equator' so the flesh can expand without bursting the skin. Break the chocolate into pieces and put into the apple cavities.

3 Place the apples slightly apart in a shallow baking dish. Pour over 125 ml /4 fl oz water and top each apple with a spoonful of honey.

4 Bake for 40-50 minutes, basting occasionally, until the apples are tender when pierced with a skewer. Towards the end of cooking, add a little more water if the honey glaze shows signs of scorching.

5 Serve the apples hot, with the honey syrup spooned over as a sauce.

time in kitchen **8 minutes**   serves **4**

total cooking time 40–50 minutes

Strawberries are blanketed with whipped cream, sprinkled thickly with dark brown sugar and grilled to a caramel crust. Other fruits – such as blueberries, sliced peaches and pears – also work well in this delicious dessert.

1 Chill the food mixer whisk and bowl in the freezer for 5-10 minutes. Preheat the grill.

2 Whisk the cream in the chilled bowl on medium speed until just firm enough to hold a stiff peak when the whisk is lifted.

3 Rinse the strawberries only if necessary. Arrange evenly in a shallow baking dish, halving any very large ones. Cover completely with the whipped cream. (Refrigerate for up to 2 hours at this stage, if preparing ahead.)

4 Scatter the brown sugar over the cream as evenly as possible. Grill as close to the heat as possible for 3-4 minutes until the sugar has melted and caramelized and the cream starts to brown. Serve at once.

Strawberry burnt cream

500 ml /16 fl oz double cream (well chilled)

750 g /1½ lb strawberries

250 g /½ lb dark brown sugar

time in kitchen **14 minutes**   serves **4**

total cooking time 3–4 minutes

Tipsy **bread** & **butter pudding**

unsalted butter for greasing
dish

175 g /6 oz day-old crusty
loaf

45 g /1½ oz seedless raisins

125 ml /4 fl oz rum or whisky

375 ml /12 fl oz milk

4 eggs

100 g /3¼ oz sugar

½ teaspoon vanilla essence

Good bread and butter pudding depends on the bread – it must be a day or two old, dry and chewy. Plenty of crust is important because it adds colour as well as texture. Opt for a French baguette, Italian ciabatta or simply a good home-made loaf.

1 Preheat the oven to 190°C/375°F/gas 5. Butter a 1.5 litre /2⅓ pt baking dish.

2 Tear the bread into 2.5 cm /1 in chunks and place in a large bowl with the raisins. Pour on the rum or whisky and two-thirds of the milk. Squeeze the bread chunks with your hands so they fully absorb the liquid, then leave to soak.

3 Whisk the eggs, sugar and vanilla together in a large bowl just until smooth. Whisk in the remaining milk. Pour this custard over the bread and stir gently.

4 Spread the mixture in the prepared baking dish and bake for 50-60 minutes, until the custard is set and the pudding is crisp and brown on top. A skewer inserted into the centre should come out clean and be hot to the touch.

5 Serve warm, with ice-cream if you like.

Apple **bread** & **butter pudding**

Replace the rum with 125 ml /4 fl oz more milk. Add 2 tart apples, cored and diced, to the bread with the raisins.

time in kitchen **10 minutes**   serves **4-6**

total cooking time 50–60 minutes

Raspberry & chocolate fool

250 ml /8 fl oz double cream

30 g /1 oz dark bitter chocolate

250 g /½ lb raspberries

2 tablespoons kirsch or lemon juice

60 g /2 oz sugar, or more to taste

15 g /½ oz flaked or slivered almonds

few toasted flaked almonds to decorate (optional)

Tart fruit – such as raspberries, strawberries, poached gooseberries or rhubarb – is best for a fool. For added texture, this fool is layered with flaked almonds and grated chocolate. Serve with Breton Butter Cake (page 127) or dessert biscuits.

1 Chill the mixer whisk and bowl in the freezer for 5-10 minutes. Chill the cream and 4 large stemmed serving glasses in the refrigerator. Grate the chocolate on to a piece of paper.

2 Whisk the cream in the chilled bowl at medium speed until thick enough to hold soft peaks when the whisk is lifted.

3 Meanwhile, rinse the raspberries only if necessary. Purée about two thirds of them in a food processor, then press through a sieve into a bowl to remove the seeds. Stir in the kirsch or lemon juice, and sugar to taste.

4 Add the raspberry purée to the cream and fold together lightly but thoroughly; the cream will thicken slightly.

5 To assemble, one-third fill the glasses with fool. Sprinkle with almost half of the chocolate and half of the almonds, then add 2 or 3 raspberries to each glass. Repeat these layers, then top with the rest of the fool. Decorate with remaining raspberries, chocolate and toasted almonds if using. Chill for at least 1 hour before serving.

Strawberry & chocolate fool

Substitute strawberries for raspberries. Purée two thirds of them, as above. Slice the rest and assemble as above.

time in kitchen **14 minutes**   serves **4**

chilling time at least 1 hour

whites of 4 eggs

pinch of salt

250 g /8 oz dark bitter chocolate

1 orange

30 g /1 oz sugar

6 tablespoons double cream

2 tablespoons Grand Marnier or other orange-flavoured liqueur

Chocolate mousse with orange

What makes a chocolate mousse memorable is less the time and trouble taken than the quality of the chocolate used – look for one with a high cocoa solids content. You can vary the orange flavour by substituting a different liqueur, such as crème de menthe for mint, or Kahlua for coffee.

1 Bring a 2.5 cm /1 in depth of water to the boil in a small saucepan.

2 Using an electric mixer, whisk the egg whites with the salt until stiff.

3 Meanwhile, chop the chocolate and melt in a small heatproof bowl over the pan of hot water. Finely pare a strip of zest from the orange and reserve for decoration; finely grate the rest.

4 When the egg whites are stiff gradually add the sugar, whisking until you have a glossy, softly peaking meringue.

5 To make the ganache, bring the cream to the boil in a small pan, then pour on to the chocolate. Let stand for 15 seconds over the pan of hot water, then stir until smooth. Take the bowl off the pan and stir in the liqueur and grated orange zest.

6 Gently fold the ganache into the meringue. Divide the mousse between 4 mousse pots or ramekins. Cover and chill for at least 2 hours until set.

7 Decorate each mousse with a strip of orange zest and serve on individual plates.

time in kitchen **10 minutes**   serves **4**

chilling time at least 2 hours

Syllabub is a classic dessert, served chilled in glasses. It is made by whisking fruit juice, sugar and alcohol into cream; the acid in the fruit thickens the cream. On chilling, the syllabub separates slightly, forming a mousse with a sauce.

1 Chill the mixer whisk and bowl in the freezer for 5-10 minutes. Chill the cream and 4 glasses or mousse pots in the refrigerator.

2 Finely pare 2 or 3 thin strips of zest from the lemon and lime; cut into julienne strips and set aside.

3 Squeeze the juice from all 3 fruit. Measure: there should be about 175 ml /6 fl oz juice; if necessary make up to this volume with extra lemon juice.

4 Pour the citrus juice into the chilled mixer bowl and add the Cognac, sugar and nutmeg. Whisk for 5-10 seconds until the sugar starts to dissolve.

5 With the whisk at medium speed, slowly pour in the cream; it will start to thicken at once. Continue whisking for 3-5 minutes, until the syllabub is thick enough to hold a soft peak when the whisk is lifted.

6 Spoon the syllabub into the chilled glasses or pots. Cover and chill for at least 30 minutes, up to 24 hours, to let the flavours mellow. Top with citrus julienne to serve.

Sherry syllabub

For a more traditional syllabub, replace the grapefruit and lime juices with 125 ml /4 fl oz medium-dry sherry. Serve the syllabubs topped with a sprinkling of ground nutmeg or cinnamon rather than citrus julienne.

time in kitchen **14 minutes**   serves **4**

standing time at least 30 minutes

375 ml /12 fl oz double cream

1 lemon, plus an extra one if needed

1 lime

1 grapefruit

3 tablespoons Cognac

125 g /4 oz sugar

¼ teaspoon ground nutmeg

½ bottle (375 ml /12 fl oz)
sweet white wine (see right)

50 g /1¾ oz sugar

15 g /½ oz juniper berries

2 cinnamon sticks

375 g /¾ lb blackberries

White wine granita with blackberries

Sweet white wine freezes to a perfect crumbling granita, with the texture of lightly frozen snow. Choose a rich muscat wine, such as Beaumes de Venise or Montbazillac, or a rich Californian or Australian wine. Serve the granita with crisp dessert biscuits.

1 Put the wine, sugar and 125 ml /4 fl oz of water in a pan and bring to the boil. Meanwhile, crush the juniper berries. Add them to the wine syrup together with the cinnamon. Simmer for 5 minutes, then take off the heat and leave to infuse for at least 2 minutes.

2 Meanwhile rinse the blackberries, only if necessary. Strain the infused wine syrup into a shallow, non-metallic freezerproof container. Cover with plastic film and place in the freezer for 3-5 hours, until the granita is firm and snowy with crystals. The granita can be kept in the freezer for up to 12 hours; after this time it starts to lose its soft texture.

3 Shortly before serving, chill 4 large coupe or stemmed glasses in the freezer.

4 To serve, pile the blackberries into the chilled glasses. With a fork, scrape the granita into soft chunks and pile on top of the fruit. Set the glasses on plates so they do not slip. Serve at once, with biscuits on side.

White wine granita with rosemary

Omit the juniper and cinnamon. Flavour the granita syrup with 2 large sprigs of rosemary, crushed. Replace the blackberries with 2-3 sliced nectarines.

time in kitchen **12 minutes**   serves **4**

freezing time at least 3 hours

Macerated peaches

These peaches really benefit from macerating in the red wine for 12-24 hours, though they can be eaten after chilling for an hour or so. They are best served with biscotti or amaretti biscuits, for dipping in the juice.

1 Pour the wine into a serving bowl and stir in the sugar. Finely pare the zest from the lemon, twist over the bowl to release the lemon oil, then drop into the wine.

2 Add the vanilla and stir for 20-30 seconds to encourage the sugar to dissolve.

3 Halve the peaches and discard the stones. Cut each half into 5-6 slices, adding them to the wine syrup. Stir gently to mix, then set a plate on top to keep the fruit totally immersed. Chill for at least 1 hour, up to 24 hours.

4 Just before serving, taste the syrup for sweetness, adding more sugar if you like. Serve the macerated peaches in the bowl, with biscotti or amaretti handed separately.

1 bottle (750 ml /27 fl oz) fruity red wine

100 g /3½ oz sugar, or more to taste

1 lemon

½ teaspoon vanilla essence

4 large peaches (about 750 g /1½ lb)

biscotti or amaretti to serve

time in kitchen **4 minutes**   serves **4**

macerating time at least 1 hour

Breton **butter cake**

250 g /½ lb unsalted butter,
plus extra for greasing tin

250 g /½ lb flour

250 g /½ lb caster sugar

6 egg yolks

This delicious buttery shortbread can be eaten alone, or with berries or a fruit compote. It keeps well for 2 or 3 days in an airtight container. Make sure you use unsalted butter, at room temperature.

1 Preheat the oven to 175°C/350°F/gas 4. Butter a 23 cm /9 in loose-based tart tin.

2 Put the flour in a pile on the work surface and make a large well in the middle. Add the sugar and butter to the well. Set aside half of 1 egg yolk for the glaze; add the rest to the well.

3 Pinch the ingredients in the well together, with the fingertips of one hand, for 1-2 minutes until soft and sticky. Gradually draw in the flour with a pastry scraper or spatula and mix for 2-3 minutes, to form a smooth sticky paste.

4 Drop the dough into the tart tin. With clean, dampened hands, flatten the dough in the tin. Brush the reserved egg yolk and mark a lattice on the surface, using the underside of a fork.

5 Bake for 35-45 minutes, until the Breton cake is golden brown, firm in the centre and just starting to come away from the sides of the tin; don't over-bake or it will be dry.

6 Leave to cool in the tin, then unmould on to a serving plate. Serve still slightly warm, or cool.

time in kitchen **14 minutes**   serves **6-8**

total cooking time 35–45 minutes

Index